It's *Always* about the Money

Julian Caesar

ISBN: 978-1-4834-4137-5 (sc)
ISBN: 978-1-4834-4136-8 (e)

Library of Congress Control Number: 2015918345

Because of the dynamic nature of the Internet, any web addresses or
links contained in this book may have changed since publication and
may no longer be valid. The views expressed in this work are solely those
of the author and do not necessarily reflect the views of the publisher,
and the publisher hereby disclaims any responsibility for them.

Any people depicted in stock imagery provided by Thinkstock are
models, and such images are being used for illustrative purposes only.
Certain stock imagery © Thinkstock.

Lulu Publishing Services rev. date: 11/18/2015

Dedication

This is dedicated to all my peers and predecessors in the world of IT (Information Technology, for those who have been hibernating under a rock). With this writing I essentially have committed political suicide; as for my career, well, it is pushing up daises now. But that is okay. The bastards cannot kill me; I am retired. That is fine; ageism, racism, and plain ignorance run a wild within the hallowed halls of the corporate sector as crab grass grows on our lawns. Today's world of IT is in such disarray that I say let the so-called golden children of IT deal with it. Besides, it's time to retire. Only God, if there is one, can save corporate America from their greedy and misguided management philosophies.

There are still many of us in the business of IT who need employment. Many of my still employed peers have the fear of reprisal, or they just don't give a damn and have adopted the philosophy of "fight the battles you can win; otherwise, concede and go forward". However, silently you do agree with what I say. It is true: you and I have seen it. We came to the mountain, and we are living it. I am just the vessel to say it.

Some say that change is inevitable, and yes, it is. Technology shows this with neon lights as if it were playing on Broadway. However, the replacement of American workers with resources of a lesser world is not good. The rationale of a "global economy" is crap equal to Ronnie's trickle-down economics and "just say no

Nancy". Oh, yes, Bill, you inhaled and probably enjoyed the buzz. The outsourcing of IT labor is more than putting some techies out of work. We are making the future generations of Americans uneducated and unproductive couch potatoes that would rather tweet their feelings rather than be productive. The real people that should be outsourced, if truth be known, are the corporate illiterates—basically, management—who sit on their fat corporate asses.

Do not get me wrong; I do not have ill will toward any foreign resources. What I do take offense at is the outsourcing of American positions to any foreign resource when there is no regard as to their lack of skills and abilities. Coupled with the wholesale transfer of jobs is the audacious claim, by corporate mouthpieces, that they are better than us. We, the American "IT resource", see these so-called golden children of IT in our faces. We work and deal with them on a daily basis. Our management treats them as sacred and revered resources. It may appear that the foreign resource are our enemy, but no, they are not. The enemy is "corporate blue", whose insatiable greed under the disguise of capitalism must be curtailed.

I equate the process of outsourcing to the Mariel Boatlift in 1980. This was an action by the Cuban government in which they opened their prisons and other institutions and released the inmates to migrate to US shores. Yep, they cleaned house, and we were their dumping grounds. And yes, the foreign third-world nations are doing it again with the blessings of corporate pinstripes. These third-world nations have many issues, severe population they cannot support internally is but one (there's a simple solution—keep it in your pants—but I digress). The process is now disguised and called "global economy". This sounds PC and is good for Wall Street. Question: have we seen any insurance company or for that fact any other company selling their wares in these substandard localities? No, they just ravage the populace of those localities for corporate gains.

This is my view, my observations, my opinion. These are my versions of the truth. My words are not idle fodder; what I say can be backed by what I have seen or not seen in the corporate world. This is neither PC nor sugarcoated; I oppose the notion of protecting the innocent, or should I say the corporate idiots. I speak the truth as I see it, and I own up to what I say. Yep, I am not a politician wanting your vote. This is your warning. Thank you, and enjoy the ride.

Be ever vigilant, old coder of COBOL, for the ides of March are upon us.

Contents

Preface

My wife, friends, and colleagues have all posed this question to me: now that you have retired, what are you going to do? Travel, relocate to a warmer climate, fish, boat, take up photography, and do philanthropic things; I say yes to all, at least to some degree. However, now that I really do not need corporate blue for monetary sustenance, I have decided to put my thoughts, observations, and prognosis of the future down on paper. Maybe my written words will wake up the Wharton MBAs from their "Sleeping Beauty" trance.

If you choose to read this, let me state up front an important fact about me. I was in IT for over thirty years. The profession was good to me, and I to IT. I have worked for many of the major companies of this land and have made many business applications better, faster, and more complete. I never had an inclination that I would be forced out by the incompetent boobs of corporate management. My biggest fear, one shared by my peers, was being left in the dust by technological advances. I had no intention of retiring this early from my position. My wife and doctor knew that I loved what I did and would "keep on truckin".

But enough of the pity party and on with the lynching. It has been said that a job is not a job when you enjoy what you do. I did, and it was fun. To say I am bitter about today's overall business climate is like calling a hurricane a summer shower. So if you dare to proceed down this yellow brick road, you have been duly informed. As a vital footnote, I do not mince words. I do not buy into the jargon of being politically correct. As a technician, where code is black and white, this is my writing style—no double entendre here. An education by two-by-four over the head is sometimes needed to get one's point across.

As you will come to read, I am a big fan of history. History does have an eerie way of predicting the future, not with ESP but with repetition. We are creatures of habit and learn from the past. Open your eyes and ears; it is all there.

I have had some success because of my writing prowess. I have resolved issues and have made the Op-Ed pages, so I thought this was the time and place to say this. I know the current corporate regime will not like me. Who cares? I do not like them anyway, and, besides, I despise incompetence sugarcoated by the paint of being an expert. Corporate management, government, and the Catholic religion have the same, parallel concepts: they never like to have their dirty laundry exposed. Yes, emphatically yes, they have plenty of dirty little secrets, and exposing them to the public is a definite no-no. The current crop of managers, no matter the company, have all these attributes: they are overrated, overpaid, dumb as they can be, pseudo-intelligent when it comes to IT, and, last but not forgotten, greedy as all hell for dead presidents. Yes, I am outspoken, rash, and not politically correct. Some readers will agree, some will not, and some will say he's lost it or ask what he's smoking. I really do not care. I speak the truth as I see it, as crazy as it may sound; I usually hit it out of the park.

I was on assignment at a major insurance company several years ago; this insurance company sold multiple insurance lines. The powers that be that managed this company proceeded to sell off several of its lines of business, a garage sale of sorts. I openly stated that it was a bad business move to sell off several of its markets. I was reviled as a radical. Then the talking heads—you know, the pros on business who talk on business shows—said the same thing I said. Now who is laughing?

This writing focuses on the world of IT and business. Why? Because I know this world and was a major resource in it for over thirty years. No matter what you do or intend to do, this corporate global economy behavior pattern can and does apply to all of us. I have seen numerous positions given away to foreign enterprises, all for the sake of the "global economy". Why? Do we need to ask? The fallout of this "nuclear" employment war will be great and will be devastating to all. Take this to heart: the fall of the American worker is imminent. Be wary of pulling your pants down and becoming Bubba's girlfriend in the vernacular and biblical sense. What a gift from corporate management! Dream on, little ones.

It brings up the question: why? Why change this so-called good thing for the American economy? The current talking heads are touting the global economy philosophy as a good thing. Remember, oh little one, smoking cigarettes was once revered as a stylish and a good thing. Why care? What good can come from this? Right you are. As I said, I am a fan of history, and I do not like what I see coming, nor do I believe in the "tradition" excuse that is always used by the elders. Nor do I presume that our talking heads in Washington are speaking the truth, so help me God. I am a cynic. I presume that is a product of age. I do not know or care.

We can and we must change the tide of current events; otherwise we will become a nation of couch potatoes. Many years ago I chose this profession, I like this profession, and I am damn good at it. Technological careers are needed and should stay here and not be given away. Technology is the way of the future. Current corporate culture is squandering technology away to inferior and substandard countries. Yes, I am a racist here, but I am an American first and foremost. I am a capitalist and not a socialist. Businesses can and do whatever they must to make a better widget, but be wary of what you wish for. The end results are attainable, but are we ready to pay the piper and sell our collective corporate souls to the devil?

I have said and will continue to say that I am an advocate for the American IT professional. I will call out and fight against the wrongs and greedy philosophies of corporate management. I had a great professional life, one that should be available ad infinitum here for future generations. So, yes, I despise the current corporate cultural behavior of the wholesale use of non-American resources. The last time I checked, this is America. My vengeance of the pen may appear to some to be misguided. But it is what I see; it is what we all see. The true enemies are the incompetent corporate execs. These executives should be exiled from upper management to a life sentence of menial labor.

I have thought long and hard about what I have written. I am poignant, definitely offensive, and most likely will not make any positive inroads to foreign affairs. The "golden children of IT" of whom I speak are a conglomeration of third-world and lesser nations of the Middle East, Asia, and beyond. I have not singled out any particular third-world country. However, those of us who are in the world of IT know of whom I speak. To continue in this same vein, this practice of outsourcing is not unique to any particular business, company, or government within our shores. This is a universal epidemic that must be eradicated, or else life and existence as we know it will not exist. I did considered toning my language down, but I know this topic is far too important to sugarcoat it to appease the bleeding hearts among us. Also I have encountered way too many non IT folks out there that really do not know how bad this problem is. I make no apologies. I make no excuses. My observations are based on reality and what I have seen with my own two eyes. This is not G-, PG-, or X-rated but definitely R-rated.

On another note, my racial, ethnic, and assorted non-PC attacks will offend. Fuck off. I have been at the other end my whole life. I have been criticized about my weight, my nationality, and my name. I have had ageism, racism, and sexism used against me. This bullied soul, well, he is not going to take it anymore; the line in the sand has been drawn, and I am going to cross it with vengeance. I do not know, only assume, that you have been probably been verbally abused or been abused in some faction. Don't you just want to stick it to those SOBs? You, your kids, or probably you know somebody that have heard what I have written, and more than likely have already said it. I feel "what goes around comes around" will make you better. It's seasoning for the soul.

1: In the Beginning

The revolving door of history is more than documented and portrayed by the following. The Vietnam whatever and the Middle East debacle have weary parallels in politics, social issues, failures, and warfare strategies. Our president during the Middle East fiasco, Georgie Bush, the kid, said that it wasn't so. Bullshit. Since when do politicos and talking heads speak the truth? Here is why I say this:

- Both were military actions. It was war, not some euphemistic line of bullshit—no matter the attempts to call the use of military action a "non-war" and using terms like *police action* or *advisors*. Are we that naive? There's too damn much PC rhetoric. War is hell, and people die in war. Do not market war as a day at the beach at Club Med.

- Both were unpopular with the Americans, with the world, and, of course, with the foe.

- Both were failures with regard to us, the Americans. The people we were trying to rescue never got fully liberated, and we paid way too much with the loss of American lives. What were the prizes of war, and were they worth it? Deaths and injuries were way too many for our people. The question still on the table is, did we accomplish anything meaningful? I think not.

- Both military actions included part-time soldiers or young draftees—basically minimally trained.

- Both had enemies who were not clearly defined. I am probably jaded by WWII accounts: the Germans had those ridiculous helmets, and the Japanese had their ethnic appearance. Vietnam had the South Vietnamese fighting their brothers of the north, commonly called the Viet Cong. Looking at them, side by side, you could not tell. Same with Iraq. It was a massive civil war, tribe versus tribe. Two movies show this: *Good Morning, Vietnam* and *American Sniper*. Both provide a glimpse of what our military had to fight against. The enemies were real; the reason for them being an enemy was there. However, why do we have to be the savior of lost causes? The reasoning for Georgie Bush to attack had merit when it started; Osama bin Laden attacked us. But the war changed direction when we could not achieve our objective. Yep, all done to save face.

- Both military actions were managed—no, *mismanaged*—by nonmilitary resources.

- Both situations saw atrocities committed by our military. The liberal pundits say this is so. I say war is hell, and collateral damage does happen. So be it.

- In both cases, many people asked, why were we really there? Simple: economics is the bottom line and final answer. War does produce profits for the few, during or after, and money is the reason. Money is always the reason.

- In both cases, the standard line from leaders about why we were there fighting was "They are fighting for your freedom." I'm confused. I was not oppressed. I was not attacked. I was living my life as I saw fit. Yes, these areas had issues that I opposed, but they were thousands of miles away in other lands. In situations like Pearl Harbor, 9/11, and attacks on an American establishment overseas, then, yes, wipe the oppressors off this world. Other than that, as

I see it, do not say they are fighting on my behalf. Or is our government proactive?

- In both cases, a question to ponder is: isn't the United States as guilty as the oppressors by imposing our style of government over what they have had for years? Is our system any better? Yes, theirs is bad, but must we forcibly initiate a change to ours? Look at our so-called statesmen. Are they role models?

History does provide us with lessons, if we just open our eyes. When we look back at historical events, we have always had twenty-twenty eyesight; the invention of the automobile shows us this. People were shocked that their loyal horse or horse and buggy were replaced by the automobile. This mechanized horse was noisy, spouted smoke, and did not need oats but a liquid fuel to run. The auto gave us many things, including additional mobility, many offshoot businesses, economic growth, gridlock, pollution, road rage, and accidents. Products of this invention—for that matter any invention—are neither all good nor all bad. However, we can all say that all progress has its costs, but the ends do justify the means sometimes.

As with anything, there is always a beginning. This is true about all businesses, all endeavors, everything. A business is a living, breathing entity that cares for one thing: itself. In other words, business is narcissism to the nth degree. All businesses, with varying intensities, are selfish, egotistical organisms that are constantly evolving, in metamorphosis, and growing. A business does not stay dormant; if it did, it would die a most certain death at the hands of carnivorous competitors. Tradition is good, but change is constant and certain. In other words, businesses are works in progress.

The advent of IT was initiated by businesses' rate of growth. Faster growth rates, expanding LOBs, more productivity, doing more for less, and being the best are all attributes a business needs to survive. The insurance company that sold insurance, recorded premiums, paid claims, and paid commissions is still doing so, except that they are doing those things faster, more accurately, and with more or less labor. The beginning era of the mechanized world of business was spearheaded by the computer. It was a new day for business, from paper and pencil to tubes and screens. A black box, a mysterious electric contraption with wires and lights, as early science-fiction movies depicted, was the dawn of electronics in the business world. The computer is a geeky thing, a scary thing, an introduction into a new world. Whatever it started as, it has evolved and re-evolved business processes to help and grow business.

Looking back, the computer was a great invention, an innovator. But take heed—progress does cost and IT was not immune from it. In the world of IT, the computer and its self-appointed handlers, the programmers and analysts, have created their own demise. Do not get me wrong. This is not a disease of habit or substance, not self-inflicted; it was hiding, disguised, and not even a blip on the radar. Was there foresight? Could this have been vaccinated against? Or was this an evolution of business? The story continues.

2: The Three Amigos—Make It *Four*

There are several aspects of life's journey that support the "consistency factor," albeit working with, against, and for you.

Death

Death is the first constant—a pleasant thought, but appropriate. Yes, man does have a definite and finite shelf life. Everybody, everything living, has a beginning, a middle, and an end; the only question is when the final curtain call is made. This is a given fact; the journey or life's longevity is the only variable. Death is the final answer to all. Is this the whole story? I say it brings more questions to the table than it answers. We all know that, as man or woman, our life begins at birth. Conception is not the issue—in your bedroom, on a tryst at a local hotel, in a test-tube commingling of egg and sperm in some clinic's lab, or in the back seat of your love's '55 Chevy. Sperm met egg, and slam-bang, thank you, Mama, we have conception. Houston, we have propagation!

As man or woman, we know and realize—although it is not thought about constantly—that our time on earth has an endpoint. Does the pig know that he is being stuffed with food for the sole reason of being slaughtered to become the bacon with our eggs? As for the veggies we buy or grow to consume, do the plants know of their demise at the first frost? Why is it that we know our ultimate fate and, I presume, nothing else does—or do they? Communication between man and animal, plant, or other organisms is at best very, very, very infantile.

We know our own personal beginnings—our parents, our grand-parents, and so on—but how does this game of life begin? I do not care if you subscribe to the theoretical or anecdotal notion of Adam and Eve with the evil serpent and that enticing apple. Or man evolving as a mutation from apes. Maybe it was some cosmic kind of big bang theory or a mixing of other theories or combinations of philosophies. Where, when, who, or what started this chain reaction called life as we know it? What are our roots? I am Catholic, not practicing but indoctrinated through years a bullshit. Given that I was told I (or should I say *we*) came from Adam and Eve, great. Where did *they* come from? The religious answer is God. Okay, who is this thing called God, this being, this force, or whatever, and where did he or she or it come from? Before calling me a heretic, an atheist, you must agree these are all valid questions. I am in systems, and a core aspect of systems is logic. I do not see the logic or path; all I hear is "take it on faith." I am a person who evaluates probabilities. I can pretty much say, with high probability, that man did not create the world as we know it. Is man capable of destroying it? Yes. Building it? No.

The constant question of philosophers is *what is the meaning of life?* Theories, arguments, thoughts, whatever—they all abound within the mind. In my opinion—yes, my opinion—this thing called life is a cruel joke. Based on what we know and acquire, in terms of knowledge, why would we be born only to die? The piggy dies to supply food and the same with veggie plants, but man? Yes, man kills man all the time, but cannibalism is rarely the reason. Enough of this philosophical jargon; this is for others to ponder and debate. My point is that death is the logical and constant end of an individual's life.

Taxes

The next pillar of consistency is taxes. Here we go again; it's always about the money. Oh, yes, no matter, the town, the state, or the country, they all want a piece of your ass—sorry, I mean your money. Now, I am not an individual saying that taxes should be abolished; however, the management and spending practices of governmental bodies should be examined and reviewed by competent and unbiased auditors as opposed to the village idiots on Capitol Hill. In life, death, and everything in between, your actions have been equated to dead presidents, and the powers that be want their fair shares. So pull down your pants, bend over, and, well, take your medicine. Taxes will continue and will continue to grow like a well fertilized and watered plant. Yes, to be consistent is to be regular.

Change

The concept of change is our next "Greek god". We, as a people, love consistency. Good, bad, or indifferent, we relish sameness. Change is the anti-Christ. With the boringness of consistency and sameness, life as we know it is on autopilot. We like that.

Go into a Mickey D's, and that Big Mac tastes the same at your local fast food joint as at the franchise three thousand miles away. People like sameness, get in a routine, stay in that routine, and put life on autopilot. Sorry, folks, this is your captain speaking. Put on your seat belts. We are experiencing turbulence; please be seated. Well, this is life. Now that we know that life is in a constant flux, man must deal with it. How he deals with change will determine how happy and healthy he will be.

Dealing with or reacting to change does not mean violence, though that is a path. Apathy is an approach, verbalization another, and of course action. All concepts are effective and food for the soul. Whatever floats your boat is your defense mechanism. There are no right or wrong approaches, no pattern of when or how changes occur; all that is known is that change always happens and change is always constant. How an individual deals with it, with an eye to his or her own benefit, is the right way for that individual. Deal with it.

It's Always about the Money

Taxes are very intimate with money; however the money relationship is polygamous. Be it crime retribution, untimely death, a sports contract, litigation, anything, it can and is always rectified with money. Yep, the "dead president quotient" is alive and kicking in everyday life. The common denominators are our old friends President George Washington, President Abraham Lincoln, Secretary of the Treasury Alexander Hamilton, President Andrew Jackson, and President Ulysses S. Grant, to state a few examples. The world of business has grasped this concept with "gorilla glue".

All the attributes discussed above are common to the business model. A business is started and lives. A business dies when competition or mismanagement kills or consumes it. The tax man cometh—he always does. No entity is immune from Caesar's greedy tentacles. Then there is change. Change is an ever-present factor in the business world. How a company deals with changes will be the deciding factor in the business's fate. And not to be left out of the game, "it's always about the money"; yes, the new "god".

3: Ten Commandments of Corporate Blue

I am neither religious nor heathen. I believe in what goes around, comes around. Maybe its karma and we get our just desserts. The concept of "commandments" is a good analogy for understanding how business works, all businesses. MBAs from Harvard or Wharton will disagree; usually the educated elite have their asses and eyes on the purist and theoretical view, seeing businesses as gods of the world. I am a skeptic, a realist, and I take my knowledge from actual observations of the day-to-day workings in the corporate sector. I take my positions from what I see and read in the real world and not the theoretical.

I am fairly good at the track (the thoroughbreds—horses, you fool). The novice who puts a two-dollar wager at the track has no blessed idea about what to do or how to do it—gamble, that is. Many of them bet on the horse's name or the color of the jockey's silks, but these factors are not pertinent in making an educated wager. Those factoids are only for dramatic interest in the movies. These bettors are better off drinking their mint juleps from their comfy couches at home. I look at the horse's lineage, the jockey's performance, the trainer, past performance, medications, length of race, weather, and track conditions, to name a few factors in making my decision. I place no particular order or weights on the individual factors; rather, the "whole information" is considered in my decision, the

9

totality of information. This is the Gestalt school of psychology; look at the totality of the parts, not individual aspects.

Business is similar. Understanding business requires understanding its rules, its commandments. This is the totality of corporate existence. Strict adherence to the commandments assures the business survival. These commandments are what I perceive and have seen to be true. The commandments are not carved in granite or written on antique parchment in some museum. They will not be listed on any stone tablet, book, or any institution of higher learning. They will not be taught, at least not explicitly, but inferred constantly by the professors of business theory and life. These character traits of a business are what I have deduced by observation and the actions and reactions of pertinent factors of all businesses. Make your own call. Here they are:

I

The business is number one. Anything done by, to, or about the business is for the business's supremacy. All other factions are secondary and expendable.

II

The primary and for that matter the only purpose of a business is to make a profit. Increasing stock price and raising the projective earning quotient are intrinsic to the calculation. Nothing else matters.

III

People are expendable, all people. That means labor, the customers, the suppliers, governments, any and all. People represent costs that are detrimental to the business. Commandment number three has a definitely a paradox, for without people buying the product of the business, then there would be no business.

IV

The product of a business is secondary. The product of a business should be good enough, but not too good. The product must have a defined shelf life and use life. When the product is released, it should allow for the creation of multiple versions or replacement by new versions; this is the "new and improved factor".

V

Fairness to anyone or anything is not doable. Destroy the competitors by any and all cost and by all means. Business is war, and war is hell. Yes, there will be casualties.

VI

Business does not need nor want any laws. Laws disrupt the activities of a business and create extra and unneeded costs for the business. We all know what costs equate to in the corporate vernacular.

VII

The laws and regulations that are on the books will be dealt with using the following approach: bend, break, or whatever. If the business is said to be guilty of an infraction of these laws then deny, lie, and cheat. What is paramount to any business is that a law is not broken if you are not caught. Laws represent unneeded or warranted costs to the business.

VIII

The people who are employed by the business must sell their souls to said business without reservation. The converse is not true. That is to say, there are no guarantees about how the business shall treat employees in return.

IX

Business is amoral. Right, wrong, ethics, morals, and feelings are not the business's concern. The business is right, no matter what; at all costs, get the job done.

X

What about me? There are no other factors, people, anything and everything, it's only about the business and what the business wants and needs. I presume the rhetoric and concept of being PC is nonexistent here in the land of corporate America.

If when reading these commandments, you find them harsh, conceited, biased, and one-sided, well, then, you have graduated and earned the coveted MBA. Look at the current business world. We have OSHA, EPA, DEEP, child labor laws, taxes, and all kind of rules and regulations. Why? A business does what it wants, whenever it wants, so help me God. An example of this is the dumping of waste, by our businesses, in our rivers. For a business it's cheaper and easier to do this than to truck it away to a controlled area. Why do companies manufacture goods in poor, third-world countries? The answer is simple: lack of laws and corruption by the local governments. In other words, cost of goods, that is all. I know you will say that is capitalism. Right you are, little one. Yes, we want cheap goods, and we do not really care about what we can't see. This is the "Air Jordan" concept.

A prime example of changing something that would benefit workers and making it benefit business instead was a piece of legislation that came to fruition in 1978, this was the start of 401(k)-legislation. The premise or spirit of this law was to give taxpayers—yep, you and I—a break on taxes, albeit only deferring them to a later date, in order to accumulate retirement funds. As they say, no good deed goes unpunished, and so it was. This legislation was manipulated by the gods of business, the corporate executives, to benefit business.

I said an employee sells their soul to the business with no guarantee of a return. This will show a prime example of this commandment. Yes, the employee is paid for his services. It's the law. Benefits on the other hand are constantly being modified or better yet lessened. Why? Cost! Back to the 401(k) issue, we all know about this benefit, but do we know the truth about and intention of bout this benefit that our government provided? Do not get me wrong—I am not in bed or in love with this gang of thieves, Congress and all. They are in my opinion in a deep and intimate relationship with business. Originally the 401(k) benefit was to be an additional retirement program, a voluntary and secondary savings program to help a person in their retirement years along with corporate pensions and Social Security. Yes, that was the intent and spirit of this legislation, but it was not the vision as business saw it. Business saw a major way to cut cost significantly. Corporations could replace their poorly run pension programs with a voluntary program that made workers solely responsible for their own well-being. Cost reduction—that's the ticket.

Business in conjunction with the clowns on Capitol Hill were on the same page. Reports, studies, and analysis are nothing new. Based on their findings, both entities—corporate management and Washington—were looking into Social Security and pensions. Could they sustain what was promised? If not, what was the prognosis? How bad would it be, and when was the "cord" going to be pulled? The short story on this was that Social Security and a plethora of public and private pension plans were in the "shitter". They could not deliver what had been promised. The reasons for this are many. However, one reason is our elected leaders. Any time there is a vast pool of money just sitting there, well then, let's spend—the rob Peter to pay Paul syndrome. They instituted the 401(k) legislations for two reason—at least this is how I see it:

1. For Social Security, the analysis forecasted a foreboding financial future. Something had to be done to lessen the blow, not fix it.

2. Another pool of dead presidents had to be created. The powers that be had to fund the pet projects of the day.

So, you see, no good deed goes unpunished.

Now back to life in the corporate world. The news has reported the decline of company-sponsored pension plans, and the plans that are in force are in trouble. Why? This is a business expense that does not help the business's goals. The jury is still out as to why pension plans were and are underfunded; was it due to the companies' lack of contribution, government mismanagement, or both? Another view of this problem is that the pensions that are now in the payout phase are being drastically changed or stopped altogether. Now business is going to do the double-talk dance, but this was a benefit that they used to entice prospective employees to work for them. They want to renege on their part of the contract.

Let's consider consumer goods. We, the all-consuming public, want the newest, the best, most improved, whatever in anything we have, and business caters to this human frailty. Look at the origin of cell phones. Mobile phones have been around for many years, but because of monetary factors they were available only to the wealthy. However, over time and technology advancements, we have our famous cell/camera/video/computer/credit card/mapping/filing system all in one. Now these qualities, features, or options did not appear all at once. No, they were rolled out as the new and improved versions. And we paid for them.

4: GOP, the Elephant in the Room on Capitalism and Business

Maybe I should take my own advice and fight the battles that I have a chance of winning. Being retired, I really couldn't give a rat's furry ass about this "outsourcing-global economy" fiasco. I have my piece of the pie. This issue is a marathon of epic proportions. However, I am a person that values fair play, at least when it concerns my fellow Americans. Boy, I sound so presidential, but I digress. Also, I do think—no, I know—that is this obsession of outsourcing is too big an issue and the outcome is way more disastrous than any negative malady that has affected the United States. With that, let's continue.

Many of my friends, acquaintances, school associates, and peers of equal stature and economics have changed sides. It is rather funny how money and success changes one's view on society. I saw this with Obamacare, Social Security, and the stock market.

People who have "made it", well, they want to keep it, and they really forget their idealistic roots. Yep, they are the epitomes of capitalism. It's all about them. In their defense, they played the game and have reached nirvana. The battle cry has sounded: hooray for me, and fuck you.

Okay, I have made it; I'm retired and financially independent. Many of my peers cannot say this with any assurance. Yes, I believe in capitalism. Yes, I believe in business. And yes, there is a common ground for coexistence. Maybe I reside on Fantasy Island, maybe I smoked too much of the "wacky tobacco", or could it be the residual effects of playing football, but I do believe in fair play.

Greed does foster more greed. I am not a bleeding heart-liberal. I play to win. I root for the home team. Oh, by the way, the Americans are the home team. Do I believe in turning the other cheek? Yes, I do—to get another shot at it to put them down. I believe in superiority. That was us. We should strive to be that by any and all means.

I will not purposely abuse a foe, but if given the chance I will take every advantage I can.

So, yes, I am an elephant and a donkey. The deciding factor is the topic.

5:   Understanding

History, that tool for recording and reminiscing about the past, does have reruns and sequels. It holds a wealth of knowledge; just open your eyes and ears, and let it into your gray matter. To know where we are today, we must look at our history, maturation, or path of our once-great profession, the world of IT. As a side note, all aspects of our current life do have a history. The profession of IT as we know it began with the advent or invention of a really dumb machine, the computer. Well, then, what is this thing called a computer?

Before anyone goes to sleep or puts this book on the back burner, this is not an IBM manual with all that technical jargon. My colleagues and I have read way too many of those epic books, and we would rather not do it again—it is in the same category of having a root canal. I am an analyst, I know my audience, and I most definitely know how to communicate with all types and levels of people. I have done it very successfully for over thirty years at some of the major companies here in the states. Some techies may or probably will take offense at my juvenile definition of their god, the computer. To them, I give a resounding "fuck off!" I have worked with some of the most self-righteous nerds. Technical experience and knowledge are great; however, I can see why they are in love with the machine—no man or woman wants them. Let's get on with it.

Okay, I said the computer is a "dumb machine". Let us not be so cruel and hasty; it is not. It is a vital cog in today's technological world, and its death or demise is most certainly not on the horizon. Simply put, a computer is an electrical box with an almost infinite number of switches inside that turn off and on—no more, no less. There, now we all are computer scientists from MIT. The science fiction movie depictions of this box being wire, tubes, and lights are not that far off—well, maybe those depictions include a little theatrical embellishment, but for the most part they are very accurate. Today's computer is a box with a plethora of printed circuits, which has all the visual pizzazz of paint drying. That is all, no special electronic genies or gizmos, just circuit boards that contains a tremendous number of switches that turn off and on. Those are the 1s and 0s you see sometimes in movies or ads; that is all you need to know. So now you are a hardware guru; you know all about that scary, black box known as the computer.

Okay, this mass of electronic switches, what turns them on and off? Do we have a light switch, like the same that we have on our walls? Do we have buttons that we push? How about keys that we start our cars with? What makes this box work, you might say its beginning? It's the infamous "code" that the media and all talk about. Well then, what is "code"?

The common man probably cannot create or read code, but he can surely know and use his credit card. He knows what happens if it is declined for his purchase, and he knows the elation of buying that gift for a loved one. Everyone knows about code, the effects of bad code, and that is as far as we want to go. The average man does not have to know the basis of an "IF statement" or a Boolean call to a database. All the common man has to know about code is the following: it's a set of letters, numbers, or symbols used to communicate with the machine, a language of sorts that the programmer cavorts with and uses to get very intimate with the machine. No, this is not a deviant sexual behavior, but a programmer does have a very close, intimate relationship with this machine.

Everybody has heard of some fashion of code problems: the weatherman's models of an impending storm are not consistent, the airline's ticket system went down and you can't buy a ticket, or the Blackberry you use will not let you send an email. Code is man's feeble attempt to talk, to communicate, with the machine. Code makes the machine do something or not do something based on the switches. Code is written by the fallible man and is the impetus for making those switches work. Yes, it is the language, the action if you will, that causes the reaction of turning off and on those electronic switches. That is code in its simplest form, nothing more or nothing less.

If you listen to the business news, where they report the activity of the stock market, you've probably come across the term "automated sells or buys". This is code. The computer has code within the computer's brain—brain not as we know it, but memory. This code is a list of many conditions. These conditions are checked constantly, and if all are satisfied at the moment, then some action is done, such as the automated transaction to buy or sell a stock. This is why, in the computer world, there is no gray, only black and white. The machine does not think, at least right now. So why all the fuss about this "must-have" box? Simple: code does what someone does in real life, something like counting widgets, except much better. A person can do this, but it takes time, and the probability of errors is always high with manual intervention. What a computer has over man or genius is speed. The universal traits of all code are as follows.

- Code is the definitive answer for everything in the IT world; all is black and white.

- The computer is always fast and getting faster. Man cannot match the speed.

- Code creates consistency in how the computer does or does not do things.

- Code allows accuracy to the nth degree.

These are the assets of a computer. Here is an interesting thought: replace our court juries with computers. All is black and white, achieving the perfect outcome every time based on the facts, not emotions or intent.

Data to the computer is like fuel for your car. Likewise the code is the engine. You can drive your vehicle until your fuel is depleted. By fuel, I mean the energy you have, which for you means sleep and nourishment; in the case of a car, no gas, no drive. The computer is collecting dust when no data is fed to this electronic albatross. The lifeline of the computer is data. What is great about computers is that fat, salt, and sugar are not in the equation, but as with food for the body, the quality of the data affects the operation of the computer. A computer works with data; it takes it in, massages it or combines it, and then spits it out. There is an old but reliable saying in the programmers' repertoire: garbage in, garbage out—in other words, you can't make gold out of shit. A significant factor of data is the amount of it and its storage or where to keep it. Think of the massive file cabinets in the common office. Devices have improved exponentially. Take music; there was live music, to vinyl recordings, to eight-track tapes, to cassettes, to CDs, to MP3s, and to NANOs.

We have just looked at the life and times of hardware (the computer) and the software (the code side of the equation). Now it is time to look at the human side. As I have stated, and will state till I am dead, the computer is a really dumb machine, just on-off switches. Speed, consistency, and accuracy make this machine the valuable resource it is. Man is the master of the machine. He thinks, he reasons, he looks at all the variables, he makes the decision to do something, and he is the ultimate computer. This is what the computer is trying to emulate or mimic: man. We as humans are striving to make this machine human, but it is a monumental task. The computer works with finite choices; all is black and white. Man and the real world have taken the concept of *Fifty Shades of Grey* to the extreme.

The programmer is the ordinary, but trained resource. A trained man, creates that code to make the computer work like his brain. Many of us programmers came from college or other careers; some just stepped in it like dog shit. Whatever the path, education was needed either by book or by fire. People learned to code by figuring out what was needed to get their jobs or their bosses' job done faster and more efficiently. As with everything, there are degrees of competency, and some programmers are better than others. Also, the computer has become bigger and faster as time goes by. The world of IT has had and continues to have growth pains.

The demand is high for good programmers. A good programmer is not the geek from some kind of technological planet; he actually has to communicate with the humanoids in the business community. A programmer has to speak English, listen to the business resources, understand the issues at hand, and provide solutions for their needs and wants. The programmer has to translate the business jargon to technical jargon, the dreaded code. He has to be intimate with that dreaded box called the computer to inject that code into its blood. Sounds Frankenstein-like; well, maybe it's not that dramatic, but the code is placed in the bowels of the computer to be tested and implemented and then to work for the customer. That is a tall order, and yes, the business community wants their request done fast—like yesterday—and they want it done right. No pressure. This is the norm, not the exception.

Simple economics comes into play here in the form of the law of supply and demand, with the programmer and his services being the commodity. Remember this: the programmer's position is treated as a commodity, ever so wrongly, by the business elite. We are a piece of paper, or a pen, or gasoline to be replenished, thrown out, or replaced at the end. This is outsourcing, the actual and real concept, pure and simple.

Let me say something here. I have referred to the human side of this profession in the masculine, using "he" when writing about the human side of IT. IT is one profession in which sex is not a variable.

"He" refers to any human resource of this profession; "she" can replace "he" with the net change being zero. Parts are parts.

Back to economics, when there is shortage in a product or the quality of the product has changed, then the cost or value of that product will rise or fall. In discussing the monetary value of IT services, the programmer, or should I say the services he represents, is the product, and his salary (or hourly rate or however compensation is determined) rises or falls on these conditions. Need has and will always exist within the IT side of business. What that need is will change, but satisfying this need, it will never happen.

In the glory days of IT—yes, folks, before the advent of outsourcing—any data processing professional working at company A could cross the street to company B and take a significant bump in pay. If this resource had something that was in demand at company B, then the bump becomes significantly larger. Trust me, this played out at all companies and locations, and it was a two-way street. This was the yellow brick road, the path to Nirvana that many in IT traveled on. Corporate bigwigs knew this, but this was the "game" and they, management, were active and volatile players.

Within most if not all companies, the data processing professional was treated as royalty, or was it fear of not having enough IT talent? The IT resource was incorporated into the corporate culture just as other employees at the same company were. Employees found a division of stature and compensation. This fact was universal among all companies. Personnel were arranged in some type of class structure within corporations; data processing and business had the same classifications except there were two tables of pay rates. The IT resource always received the higher monetary amounts. The non-IT personnel did not like this "equal but different" philosophy, but this is how it was in the corporate world. I guess communicating and cavorting with R2-D2 does have its privilege—move over, American Express. Corporate management was out of control with their IT resource. The relationship mimicked George Steinbrenner and his checkbook regarding the Yankees.

Keep in mind, the folks in corporate headquarters ultimately pay for the IT services.

Reality rarely lives up to perception. Yes, monetary rewards in the IT world were there, but the day-to-day tasks that we did were not those portrayed in the media. Many non-computer professionals imagine a programmer's job as being similar to one portrayed on shows like *Criminal Minds* or *NCIS*. Yes, the computer activities performed within these shows are an arm of IT, but a very small one; most of us are application programmers. Let me explain here. An application programmer takes a business task like collecting money and posting this money to the correct accounts. The old way was to get the accounting pads out, record the dollar figures, and calculate the balance. All that manual labor translated to all that error or possibility of error within this business function. The application programmer transforms all that into code and has that nasty computer do all the tedious manual stuff, faster and accurate all the time.

Our jobs were gratifying and rewarding but far from "red carpet" glamorous. When it comes to the now-standard rite of passage of taking your daughter or child to work, if it is in the IT arena, our children are bored to tears to see what we do. If you were to see me at work, then you would see me reading code, analyzing where the data came from and where it's going, mapping data or processes, checking if the code represents what the customer wants, designing code fixes, and yes, even coding and testing fixes. We do not play games, follow money trails, or solve espionage issues, just plain business issues. Reports have to be produced on time. The online systems had to be up and running with current data for the start of the workday, or all hell would break loose. Heaven forbid we experience an ABEND (abnormal end of process or system crash), which could put the workforce into panic mode; we had our tense moments. But when we saw the fruits of our labor, it was nice, as were our payroll checks. There was a tenuous border between the computer and business world.

6: The Marriage of Figaro

Marriage of two individuals is a union of pluses and minuses, give and take, additions and subtractions, to become a single and cohesive entity, the couple. No one part of this union is greater or lesser in value to each other; they are one and act in unison as one. I do like symmetry. I do like non-conflict and equality. But that is not reality. *Fantasy Island* was a television show, not life.

Back to reality, this marriage is not holy or serene, but truly turbulent. We have two worlds colliding or joining forces: the business world and the IT world. The business world is dynamic and changing, always wanting to get a step of the competition while simultaneously getting the costs of doing business down. So, businesses, meet your new partner, the world of IT. The "IT world" of code and man, files and databases, constantly evolving, growing, and changing, and lest we forget, costly. This is the Hatfields and McCoys of the here and now. What a tumultuous couple; you might equate the affair to sibling rivalry, a real "odd couple" of sorts. It should be a mystical couple working for a common goal—the business—bringing its pluses to the table to make the business the best it can be. This couple does work for the business, but the road is rocky and has many mistresses. This is the gospel of reality as we know it.

As in any relationship, both parties are never in total agreement; thus, the compromise. For most couples this is true. However, in the business world, the couple relationship—the one between corporate management and IT—does mimic, in ways, the two-year-olds, as we lovingly call our government's Congress. The solution is an open dialog to discuss and come to mutual agreement; yeah, that's the ticket. That means both parties win and lose, but that is fine if the basis of their relationship is strong. This concept would be a total win for business, if only it were true.

Now as for the marriage of business and IT, well, fairy tales are just that: we don't live happily ever after. The business came first and assumed the role of dominant partner here—you might say "on top". Well, I guess you can assume this since IT is subservient to the business and business pays for the IT services. However, this hard and fast Mason-Dixon Line had more gray than black and white. Remember, in the IT world we have the hard-core techie; they get down with the big black box—as Olivia Newton John sang "Let's Get Physical", these folks did. But there was a major faction in IT, the application programmers. I was one of many who proudly wore the hat of an application programmer. This group worked in the trenches of the business. They worked where the rubber met the road. Here is where IT became as important if not more so concerning their position within the company. They needed to know more and more of the business details to have that little black box perform up to par. The Korean War created a DMZ or demilitarized zone at the thirty-eighth parallel. This was a place of neutrality and non-fighting, in the IT world this did not exist.

The marriage of the two partners soon developed into a *ménage à trois*. In the business sector, the control over IT was questioned. The business's power, as they perceived it, was diminishing, and they did not like this. Yes this was the intimate third player, IT control. Control, in the IT eyes, was not an issue; however business felt it to the contrary, yet they were still paying the bill.

IT departments within companies spent money, but by spending money the IT areas made the corporations better and more efficient firms. Efficiency translated to cheaper labor and materials.

However, this talk about the value of IT services made business very uncomfortable, since it added costs to the business.

For a business, monetary costs are always in the forefront and are part of an internal war that has no foreseeable end in sight. Battles and skirmishes will be won by one side or the other. The outsourcing philosophy has made monetary control paramount and the sole objective of corporate management. Also, it has given a temporary advantage to corporate management. Business knows it needs the computer to prosper and survive in the business world; while it is an expense, it is a necessary evil. Corporate management always omits or seems to forget all the economic players here. They always puts out the "golden carrots", cash to get the highly valued IT resource. The everyday, run-of-the-mill, non-IT person is an il- literate when it comes to dealing with IT, and that is fine, provided that any control they have is directed to the business side and not IT services. Corporate management does not understand and may not even know about their local technological community. This is fine, provided a trust prevails between the partners.

Instead, both sides essentially talked at, loathed, and feared each other, living in an unholy alliance and barely tolerating each other. Even though the IT resource was compensated on a higher scale, the business still called the shots. However, these business areas had this deficiency in communication, and the monetary costs of IT put management in a non-management game. Business had lost control, and business always wants to be in control. In other words, it was, in my opinion, like letting the wolves runs the henhouse.

Business did not understand IT, and really they did not need to know bits and bytes. What they needed was mutual trust, which was lacking.

This was and is the gospel according to I Bake Muffins.

7: ROI

At all companies, the computer departments spend money while the sales department sells whatever the company produces or provides—insurance, cars, investments, whatever— and brings the dollars in. The computer department is always subservient to the business departments. Why? Because the business pays for needed computer services. This is Basic Business 101.

A simple and most important factor in business is ROI, return on investment. Business looks at IT services in two ways: as a service like one has that cuts lawns and as an investment in what they do for the company. Corporate management believes and expects that every dollar they spend in IT, will be returned along with a healthy and generous dividend in sales increases, productivity improvements, or decreased manpower, which relates to cost reductions. So everything that the IT department does has to be cost justified, or it is not done. Here is where the salt meets the open wound.

There was and always will be an internal civil war within corporations between the business area and its nemesis, the IT department. This is a love–hate relationship. Business areas have always hated or better yet misunderstood the IT departments. Why, you may ask; they work for the same company. Can't we all get along? Sorry, Rodney, not going to happen.

The monetary transactions for services rendered are accounted for in two fashions: "funny money" or direct dollars. Direct dollars is real money is that actual dollars are used to pay the incurred IT cost. Funny money is a term that represents a concept used in corporate accounting to track budgets and where the departments are financially during the year. It is like your fuel gauge on your car. When you start you are "Full"; as you drive the gauge indicator creeps toward "Empty". This is how funny money works.

IT is subordinate to business, and no code is worked on, created, fixed, analyzed, or discarded without big brother, i.e. corporate management, blessing it. Along with the previous fact is this: IT work of all types continues to grow and grow within the company. Neither the economy, health, war, nor natural disaster will stifle the growth of IT work within the company. If a company goes out of business, then the IT that supported the business will continue in some fashion till there is no business. This is one profession that has no known enemies, except internal corporate management. This is the gospel according business, and it is as true as death and taxes. Now let me interject two situations when business and IT always have issues. First we have the ever-present maintenance of preexisting software.

Maintenance

As good as computers and code are getting, there will always be a need to maintain the code so it can perform optimally. The best way to describe IT maintenance is this way. Most of us own and drive cars. When we buy a vehicle, besides the nicely shined chariot and payment book, we are presented with the dreaded owner's manual. That diatribe says certain things have to be done at certain time intervals to maintain said vehicle. One of these activities is the oil change. For that you have to:

1. Make an appointment.

2. Take some time out your busy day to have some person go under your car.

3. Undo a value and release all the oil from your engine.

4. Tighten the loosen valve.

5. Put new oil in your engine, which looks exactly like the stuff that was removed.

Well, you're right and wrong. The quality of the oil removed and the oil replaced may appear the same to the naked eye, but it is substantially different. If you have the perseverance to not allow the idiot light or the visible message attached to your windshield to get to you, then you can continue driving your car for some indefinite period of time and say to yourself, "I beat the car and oil people". Well, yes, you did, but as the FRAM filter ad said many years ago, "You can pay me now, or you can pay me later". Trust me, pay it now; the later bill is a killer. IT has the same scenario.

Companies hound us all the time to buy their products—hey, this is capitalism. However, these same companies are the recipients of the same pressures. Corporations already have hardware and software, this was the "in" for the salesmen who approached corporate management. Some of the selling techniques are not so subtle and border on the hard and nasty behavior of the door-to-door salesman. This aggressive approach is fear-based to the point of threatening that the ultimate reversal of the status quo is at hand if you, Mr. Corporate do not buy my new and improved version or update to your IT arsenal. This was said to be done. Maybe it was or maybe it wasn't; however, fear of the unknown is a prime tactic of the "head game" in sales.

The situation exists in other areas, although perhaps not as dramatically. Look at your own cell phone. Every six to nine months environmental changes cause you to upgrade or better yet buy another phone. It is still happening.

Yes, maintenance, either buying new products or tweaking present code, is performed daily. It is needed, it is not exciting, but it must be done to survive. In terms of ROI, it is very hard to determine that monetary value; however, not addressing the issue makes ROI a moot point, as there would be no business.

Next, the project.

IT Projects

The IT project, whether it be a new system, an enhancement, or whatever tasks requiring business and computer worlds to work together, is always an adventure. Inevitably there are delays, unreasonable deadlines, and cost overruns leading to the dreaded finger-pointing of blame as to why this happened. I worked for many consulting companies or vendors who supplied IT resources to many companies. All had their pluses and negatives; however, I always took away some valuable insight. In this area of the business, there are two modes of business: the project, usually a fixed-bid contract for a piece of work, or time and materials, a resource assigned to do whatever is needed at an agreed-to hourly rate.

Fixed Bid project work can be very profitable for the IT consulting/vendor companies who receive the work, but it can be more deadly if the rules are not defined first. I had the pleasure of working for several of these firms. They had project work down to a science and were very profitable because of it. For example, let's say Project A was estimated to take nine months to develop, test, and implement with ten resources at forty hours per week for a cost of $4 million. This means that the project was to be delivered in nine months, working correctly. If the project was completed in seven months or twelve months, the agreed compensation was paid. It sounds like a nice plan, but be ever vigilant of Murphy's Law. Inevitably the specifications supplied to the project team had an issue or omission of key information or changes to what they wanted, leading to specification changes, thus leading to project delays. The IT firm always wanted to be on time or early, for that meant the profit was optimal. Late meant they were to pay their staff out of expected profits, which is not a good thing. Several of the companies I worked for had a clause preventing overruns and delays, a clause protecting them from monetary disaster. If the business customer changed the specifications, the agreed-upon contract would be null and void, and all the project cost estimations would be redone. The business customer, user, abuser, or whatever has not changed in the years that I have been in my profession regarding an IT project. Call it what you may, specifications are not complete, either by inadvertent omission, attempted cost savings, changes in the business plan, or just plain incompetence. All this leads to is the IT project is delayed. Not a good thing. Management of course is quick to point the fickle finger of fate at the IT department and not at themselves—after all, management is always right and infallible. Yes, Virginia, God is living and breathing in corporate pinstripes.

A significant project went on several years ago that was universal to all companies. No matter who you were or what you did, you heard the saga of Y2K. The media in its infinite wisdom and desire to be the *National Enquirer* of today's generation, perpetrated mass hysteria and fear in the general public. All their news was based on pure speculation, ignorance of IT, and innuendo that the computer world would experience Armageddon. Well, the media stirred the pot, but the laugh was on them. Nothing happened; damn, we American IT resources are good.

Let me explain the Y2K problem in Y2K for Dummies vernacular. There was a real problem. This was not an IT plot to get more dollars from companies. Why did it occur? Could it have been prevented? What was done?

Let us look at the problem known lovingly as Y2K. This will clarify the why question. Technology growth is like crabgrass, fast growing and fast spreading. In IT things are done, for the most part, for the here and now and not the future. If a questionable piece of code is installed, then the possible reasoning for it would be we will fix it later, it will be replaced, or it's temporary. Foresight is never, or perhaps I should say rarely, in vision, and it's for good reason: future technology is never known. The standing rule is get the project done now or, better yet, yesterday. Many of the systems that I have worked on were ten, twenty, thirty, forty, and more years old. They were never replaced or fixed; the adage "if it ain't broke, don't fix it" applied, not to mention the ROI factor.

A key factor of IT in its infancy was space, and this was the issue at the heart of Y2K. The amount of code and the size of data files were something the programmer had to be aware of in the "early" years. To the non-IT person, using two characters rather than four to store a date probably doesn't seem like a big issue, but let us look at the big picture. There were often multiple dates in a record, with multiple records in a file, multiple files in a system, multiple systems on a computer, multiple computers in a network ... the problem grew exponentially.

Could this have been prevented? No. A better question is, could this problem have been addressed and fixed earlier as technology allowed it? Yes, but where was the ROI? Old IT processes were still producing good results; why change them when they were working fine? As time progressed and technology improved, the areas could have been revisited and tweaked, but an IT department had a better chance of winning the lottery than convincing the finance department to spring for this kind of project. The answer was to defer a fix to a later date—after all, everything was working well.

What was the fix? This question was answered on a system by system basis; there was no general fix. I cannot recall a system with Y2K issues being "sunsetted" or retired (turned off, in laymen's terms). However, never say no systems were turned off; I assume some were, but where I was this was not done. Some date code was "windowed", buying fifty or so years. The management was hoping that a replacement of the file or database would be done. This will only elongate the Y2K problems to a future date if not addressed. The two fixes I saw used were to reorganize some databases or files and to change the area housing the date data to include full four-digit years.

As I stated, the fixes were needed; the problem was not self-inflicted purely for monetary gain. However, the media had a boring night when 1999 turned to 2000: no planes crashed, ATMs worked fine, no stores went out of business, all appliances worked fine. All in all it was a quiet night, just what business wanted. ROI was not apparent, but customer satisfaction was readily apparent. The cost of this project was hefty, the return was "goodwill", which is an asset to a business, but assigning a monetary figure to that asset is not easy.

8:   I Want to Go to Miami

People and businesses have a commonality: they are dynamic entities. They are not stagnating in a vegetative state; they grow, change, and adapt with the times. Such is also true about the IT professional and business expertise. These two groups of people have another commonality: both have no loyalties but to themselves as they progress through time. This is so very true but not so harsh. For the IT professional, money is as tempting as that apple Eve enticed Adam with. Money is an equalizer, money is the common denominator in most solutions, money is only paper (or should I say rags) that can provide its owner such resources as food, shelter, pleasure, and yes, happiness. So do not say money cannot buy happiness. Happiness is not universal; it is a subjective feeling of the individual. One person's happiness is another's hell.

In the logical progression of a person's career is advancement or promotion, money, or stability which will surely be acquired by a successful employee. The degree, amount, or intrinsic happiness is subject and dependent on the chosen career. The IT resource wants this, and the corporation knows this for themselves as well as the resource. A mobile IT resource who has jumped from corporation to corporation will often be posed a common question: where do you see yourself in five years? This is a valid question. Companies are constantly planning and forecasting; they would like to know your intentions, kind of like interrogating your daughter's date before they leave your sight. You may say the right words, but really, what are your intentions, and what are questioner's intentions?

The answer to where you see yourself in five years is simple. The company's goals is management's impetus to ask the question, not the prospective new resource. The interviewer is trying to determine if the interviewee will sell his or her soul to the devil; so will you? This may sound like a purely narcissistic approach, but it is so very accurate. And yes it is very narcissistic, as a perspective employee you must sell your soul to the company. The goal of the company will stay the same, but the course of action can and will change. The company is looking for longevity in their choice of resource. They are looking for a person who is just not going to sit behind a desk and collect a paycheck every two weeks; they are looking for a block of clay that they can mold into what they need while giving the resource only what they want to give; all in all, it's all about me. *Me* being the operative word. The corporation or company is searching for what it needs to being satisfied, not what the prospect needs. On the other hand, the prospective resource can say all the right words, but what does he really want? Money, getting away from a bad situation, a hot piece of ass, better technology, a better position, and maybe just personal advancement; one thing that was always certain, the IT resource was ready for a change in his mind. The company actually never knows and can only assume. This scenario is playing and will continue to play out at all of our casinos and in corporate America; it's called poker. Yes, poker, the game of mastering the bluff.

Attrition of personnel is as common as death and taxes, like one plus one equal two, and people come to companies as well as leave them. Companies need to deal with and adjust staff levels constantly. The IT resource is both an asset and a liability, all tied up in a nice Christmas bow, and corporate bigwigs bite their collective tongues and cringe over this fact.

Companies like to groom employees for managerial positions; the programmer becomes a team lead, a project manager, a director. Well, that is the company's side. I was like many of my peers; we enjoyed the status quo. We liked developing and making code work and all that entailed, it was like a piece of art. Many of us did not want management, or in my opinion glorified babysitting assignments. Managerial positions in companies mean endless meetings, bullshit procedures, acting as referee in personnel squabbles, and not doing what the programmer likes to do: analyze, build, and fix code.

Even though it was readily apparent to the programmer, the common, everyday programmer would be a great manager if only dealing with IT issues. This programmer knows the ins and outs of systems. He knows code. He knows databases. He has performed analytical tasks. He has decent project management skills, and if he has been in the business long enough he has the business analyst skills to work with the customers of IT. However, there is a negative side to staying on the technical side, or at least the corporation perceives this to be a problem: nobody within the present IT area wants to step up to be an IT manager, and that void has to be addressed for the business.

There was an article in an IT magazine, a trade journal of sorts, many years ago, with the title "Be Careful, Your Next IT Boss Will Not Have IT". At first I paid little attention, if any, to this article. I guess a laissez-faire attitude had settled in. As spring turns into fall, however, I can attest that my views have been altered dramatically. I cannot say this more emphatically: this title and the article are as sure and accurate as death and taxes. I have been interviewed by, worked for, and supported the current IT management, all of whom are totally illiterate when it comes to that "black box". The vast majority of my peers, I dare to say, preferred keeping their hands dirty in code, the management shortage did continue, and so corporate America went to Plan B. Companies hired IT managers directly out of school with little, if any, IT exposure, neither theory nor practice. They put them in some sort of PM (project management and its life cycle) training and let them loose. It was kind of like having wolves manage the henhouse. The theory of a little bit of knowledge is so dangerous in the untrained person was proven categorically to be true. These new classes of managers are the dumbest and most egotistical people I have had to deal with. First, you cannot speak to them about anything remotely technological; they have no blessed idea what you are saying and have no idea what they should question. Second, as for PM, many don't seem to understand this well-known IT proverb: nine women simultaneously pregnant for one month do not a baby make. In other words, if we can complete a project in nine months using one resource, putting nine resources on it does not necessarily mean we can get it done in one month.

This new class of managerial idiots is why we have Agile instead of Waterfall philosophies. For those who missed, that let me explain. These are two schools of philosophy regarding how to run an IT project. A project or enhancement has a proven, defined path from getting the business requirement to implementation. The tried and true approach is called the SDLC, or systems development life cycle. There are two philosophies on how to do this: Waterfall and Agile. Waterfall is older and is a top-down approach. Everything that is done in the Waterfall philosophy is needed to proceed to the next step. You keep building on what has been done. Yes, there are variations and pitfalls, but they will always exist. The project will be installed and accountable to a budget. Agile is the brainchild of the new age of business people who, for lack of a better term, have developed a CYA process to cover their collective asses, their inadequacies. Every process, report, screen, anything, is broken down into entities that are worked on independently during an IT initiative. A screen is worked, re-worked, and re-worked. The Agile process mimics driving your car on a frozen lake—your tires keep spinning, but you are getting nowhere. An "IT initiative" never gets implemented; the project team keeps going back for more and more specs, all the while never implementing a thing. You've got to love this productivity; the customer has gotten the monkey off their back on being thorough, and they have a free "get out of jail" card. I have yet to see an Agile-run project come near to the all-famous budget, and I'm sure I never will—it's the "open checkbook" way of doing business now.

I have talked to many seasoned IT folks, and they are in agreement that Agile is the smoke-and-mirrors approach to doing their job. Many of the current IT folks who are still gainfully employed have reverted back to the tried and true Waterfall methodology. But the problem of incompetent IT management still exists and is still spreading its deadly philosophies.

The next, and probably the most important, aspect is the grasp of concepts. Many of us in the business have seen and dealt with similar problems or issues in our tenure, and we have gathered and stored good and bad solutions, situations, and other thoughts that can and should be applied or considered for the task at hand. The new class of manager does not get this. This class of idiots thinks they have invented something unique. Another way of looking at this is, ignorance is bliss.

This quality of the new IT management has brought the use of matrixes and bean counters in at micro levels for their position. IT resources are compared purely at the theoretical and not the functional level. Yes, many IT resources have the same technology, same business, same experience, and same exposure; however, they are still vastly different. The new regime has equated them as equal, and this has caused major strife in the IT employment ranks. I will expound on this later.

9: I Can Do That

To the untrained eye and mind, any professional can make their profession look easy and make it seem that the fuss about them is purely hype. A PGA golfer hitting his ball on a nice sunny day, somebody singing live at a concert, or a baseball player hitting a home run may all appear to be doing something easy. Bullshit! Look at a pro golfer at a televised event. He stands at his starting point to tee off. He hits the ball down the narrow fairway avoiding the sand, the rough, water, and scores of fans and spectators. Yes, it looks easy. He has dealt with all these factors and hit a perfect shot. As with most things, there is more to the story. With the ball on the ground, he takes several warm-up swings, approaches the ball, adjusts his stance, and then swings away. This view is at the thirty-thousand-foot level, and yes, the ball sails to where he intends it to go. No pressure; it looks easy. Hey, it's not football where a linebacker wants to send you into next week or baseball with an intense pitcher throwing a rock at your head at 100 mph for you to hit with a piece of wood. It's just the golfer and the ball, pure poetry in motion. Now let's get down to reality. Hours and hours of practice, the many buckets of balls he has hit at the practice tee, the many small details his body must execute in the right order and style to get the desired hit, and the discipline he imposes on his mind to shut out the crowd and their peering eyes looking for good and sometimes a disastrous shot. Sure, it looks easy; he is a pro, a well-trained and practiced pro, who delivers what he has trained for, and we are all in awe and amazement.

Now the computer programmer, who deals with a techie, who talks business-eeze, who writes a non-coherent (to non-IT humans) machine language that communicates with the "big black box", is not as glamorous or as well compensated as a movie star or professional athlete. Still, he has pressure to perform at his "A" game all the time. Time deadlines, service-level agreements, company perception, product delivery, and sometimes life and death may depend on his performance. My employment might appear to be mundane and boring. It's a position where "take your child to work" would be hell for the kid. A well-seasoned IT professional who embarks on his given task does the following. He gathers the needed information from a multitude of sources. He performs an assorted array of analyses to find the missing pieces, which there always are. He evaluates the findings for review and presentation to confirm that business and IT are on the same planet. Now is when the IT resource creates his magic and pulls that rabbit out of the hat. He translate the English language into the mysterious code, tests the code, installs his masterpiece, and implements the solution. All this is done without fanfare, just diligence and the knowledge that solutions are attainable. And yes, this code must be on the money; there is no margin for error.

Corporate management was observing the IT performance of their IT staff. Although they saw the results and observed the IT resource in action, they did not fully understand. Still, they were poised to take action, and they did. I had an experience at a major defense contractor that shows this stupidity. Any corporation that wants to do business with the government, particularly the military, wants to get a jump on its competitors, and so did this one. The company hired a director of IT, not a significant concern for IT staff. They got their candidate from the retired military ranks, a general. This general had no previous IT exposure, which was okay; he was a high-ranking military man. The company had his work and assignments all planned out. This was a quick path to the business at the military, a good thing for a defense contractor. His corporate position, Director of IT, was a safe haven where he couldn't cause too many problems and was considered just a token position—at least, that was the plan. All corporations are inundated with products from IT software and hardware companies, everything touted as needed to make their company's IT department better, faster, and more cost efficient. The salesmen of these firms, well, to put it mildly, could be the new and improved snake charmers of the Wild West or modern-day used car salesmen. The claims and virtues of the salesmen's products might be valid, but as they say, buyer beware. The usual course of events on a visiting sales call is as follows. Management is there (hey, they are writing the check) along with some of the company's IT resources, who are there to evaluate the sales pitch. The sales pitch needs to be considered, the salesmen needed to be questioned on his product/services he was selling, the products examined, and an assessment made on what they have heard and seen as to how their current IT departments will be affected. That is usually the approach, the prudent approach. In this case, however, this protocol of joint management and technical resources just did not happen; the "token", as he was referred to, and his ego were front and center. This token general assumed the position and, as they say, no good deed goes unpunished; management bought the farm. What should have taken place did not. Management bought the product without guidance from IT. Yes, the product did what it said it would, but a sledgehammer was needed to get it in and maintained. Net results: the old systems were far less costly than the new one. Too bad, for there was no back-up or recovery in the plan; they were beyond the point of no return.

Corporate management always has an issue with the costs incurred by IT services. You might say it's due to the programmers' greediness for the dollar. Yes, but do not leave management as totally blameless. MLB has gone through some labor issues revolving around revenue and salaries. My position on this is that if management placates players by raising salaries, then the responsibility lies with management. In this game as well, management put all kinds of dollars on the table, and the programmers took the money. What type of individual wouldn't? Now management is crying foul? No way.

This same token IT Director also got the idea of outsourcing the IT department as a cost-savings ploy. It was not. It was a behavior in futility, splitting business and IT further apart and making no business gains. Monetarily savings were not recognized.

10: Are We There Yet?

There has never been an official declaration of war, but the love-hate relationship between the business areas and the IT department is ever present. The elephant in the room is flourishing. At the companies where I worked or consulted, the line of demarcation, though invisible, was as blatant as the corner stop sign. It was unspoken, yet you saw and felt the tension. It was real. It was there. IT services are like a person on drugs; the first "hit" might be free, but the mind and body want that fix ever more and more. IT is here now and even more so here to stay.

Corporate management needs the services provided by this black box, and they need results as of yesterday. Even though the relationship between IT and business has existed for a long time, corporate America is still at odds with IT. Time has not educated, primarily the business community in the ways of IT, or understand what and how IT does its magic, or economically substantiate IT costs, or finally trust the IT area. Plain and simple this is sandbox 101, play with all the kids and make nice. Yes this is one sided and it should be. IT is the invited, we are guests to business. Business management has the money. And yes, IT is making their positions better. Corporate management has a superiority complex; well, they do ultimately pay the bills. Typically, management types think they are infallible; they never look at themselves as part of the problem. They assume that since the computer is a fast tool, the coding that makes it fast should also be fast to create. Sorry,

Charlie. Computer programming is like Chinese cooking: while it takes only a short time to cook the food, it takes a long time to prepare the food for cooking.

Perception and control of the IT departments and resources by an uneducated business resource has disastrous results at best. Ask any IT professional, and you will get the same answer: give me the specs, let me analyze and check the options, and we will develop a plan to do it. This takes time. *Takes time*, the most disturbing words heard by business management from their IT resources. They want it now, better yet yesterday, and yes, it must be spot on. As I said, *no pressure!*

Within the realm of IT most things can be done. Those things that cannot be done today, will be available tomorrow. Those things that can be addressed in the world of IT have only two requirements: time and money. IT is not the exception here; it's the rule. Technology is growing at astounding rates; things that were once difficult have become second nature, and management wants more and more for less and less. But the question IT has for business remains the same and will continue forever: what do you want? The computer programmer needs details. It is the nature of the beast, the computer, which is all about the black and white, to need specifications. Specifications, not assumptions, not "what if", but hard and fast rules that are the basis of the code.

I have talked to business personnel at all levels. Management, for the most part, always talks at the thirty-thousand-foot level and not at the ground, where IT is. They either have a problem defining what they want or are clueless when it comes to the details and logic needed to get there. I have spent hours asking questions to get details, yes, details. I remember going into a travel agent and saying I want to go on vacation; what can you show me? The travel agent was flustered, and rightly so. She needed more details about what I like, dislike; what I want to do; whether I want to be active, inactive, hot or cold; whether I want a party atmosphere or just peace and quiet. It is the same with systems work—the product is in the details. Computers can't think, at least for now. There are significant roads being made into artificial intelligence, but to the application programmer that option is not available yet. So it goes back to the user, the abuser, the customer: what the hell do you want? Once those questions have been answered and defined, the next question—I mean *demand*—is always, when can I have it? The perception of speed is in the mind of the customer. Do not forget time is money, and IT spends money.

With the proliferation of more and more illiterate IT management, propagated by a dysfunctional corporate culture, the old, but still valid statement exists which is. It is that a little knowledge is a dangerous thing, can be said without reservation. The balance of power was never in question, except now the tightrope walker is without a net. The stakes are raised past the house limits. Understanding an IT professional's job, databases and file structures, and some kind of logic and analysis is paramount, but it is not on the horizon for corporate management. Money is always an issue.

The local bean counters and their cost analysis matrix are in the forefront. The perception these bean counters have of what IT does is ludicrous. The snake oil jargon, perpetrated by business management, is that foreign, substandard IT resources are the computer's new and empowered masters of data processing. Corporate America has been sold the idea—or has developed it with their own gray matter—that the foreign resource is far superior to the American. How can this be? Look at it logically. Third-world resources, from mediocre to poor environments, are far from technology gurus. Their education system is questioned by us, yes Americans. I have been asked to prove my college degree. This is a first and well caught me off guard. I asked the person, who posed this, how? Why? And that this is a first after many years in the business. I was informed that this is an old habit, you are American from an American school, so it is not an issue. However foreign worker's credentials are suspect. With that statement, how are they better than us?

If these third world IT guru's education is suspect, then how can they be considered better workers? IT is not inherent, training is required. However technical training is far from being enough, business knowledge is needed. This aspect is through experience or training. These foreign resources have no business expertise and what I have seen not quick learners. So how can they be better than Americans?

Working with and honing our business and IT skills are the experiences that business wanted when they hired us. With many years of exposure and experience within business, the American IT resource has become not just a techie that works with that electrical marvel; it has gained more and more business knowledge. The present business management have become obsolete. R2-D2 is taking over.

Corporate management feared for their existence, fueled by their abundance of ignorance and lack of self-esteem. In today's world of technology, the pure business manager often has no expertise with the computer, and this invokes fear and anxiety. Corporate executives have an issue of self-preservation, so they thought. They have deemed the inept Middle Eastern, Asian, and other associated third-world kingdoms' technical resources, the so-called golden children of IT, and the "savior" of IT services. The executives want and need their computer services yet want to eliminate the cost, the high cost they created. However, something more than cost reduction was achieved: control and total authority over the kingdom. By outsourcing corporate management had the IT puppets by the marionette strings, and there was no opposition. The American IT resource was replaced with a nonassertive player, and that was what corporate executives ultimately wanted. In reality, the henhouse is controlled by the wolves.

Business areas still have not addressed a universal problem. That problem is completely and clearly spelling out what they need. Business has instead used the bullshit line of blaming IT overrun costs and delays on the IT department; it's always the other guy's fault. But if management wants control, then it must take the responsibility. This is what we say to our teens when they start driving; take heed, for this philosophy applies here, too.

Control of IT was and still is corporate management's ultimate goal. Actually, regaining the perception of the physical control was the prize. Yes, a major head game was played on one part of corporate America by another part. Control over IT resources had never been lost—business always had the checkbook. However, with the introduction of the computer to everyday business life, corporate executives had no real control over a subordinate area, the IT area. Corporate management did not need to micromanage IT but to trust and coexist with IT. Yes, they pay the salaries, authorize work, and get resources, but day-to-day management is not attainable. Most people in corporate management do not understand "bits and bytes", what the tasks at hand are, why we do what we do, and why timing and order of tasks are important; they just do not understand or know this. Why? They are not or have not been trained in this area, nor should business need to understand the many miniscule details of IT's daily routine. They know the business they support, the processes of getting their work done, the outside intervention of other resources, the deliverables they need to create and for whom. But how does IT do it? That is the sixty-four-million-dollar question. The answer to this issue is simple: trust. As with any relationship, trust is the cornerstone of the foundation. Without trust you have anarchy. IT intimidates the non-IT; the business side, in some respect, spikes fear and anxiety in some on the IT side. However, corporate management has taken back the "control" of IT, with outsourcing being the means. Even though the nationality or origin or the IT resource has been changed, corporate management will realize over time that the same tasks that were once done, but not understood, will continue to be done. I will go on record to say that the costs of said maintenance will increase substantially. So have corporate executives achieved their ultimate goal? I think not!

All businesses are amoral and not charitable. Do not be fooled by charity events where a corporation presents a substantial check to the host. It is done for perception. It is done on camera in front of a large audience. Essentially it is an advertisement, a "goodwill" gesture, but everything done by a business is for the business.

Everybody and everything have their price. Business is solely about the "what about me?" factor. You have to love American genius and good old capitalism.

One of the major costs within any business is labor. You do not need a Harvard MBA; just look at anything you have done. Let's say your car needs a repair. The bill is broken down into two major categories: parts and labor. The labor portion is always significantly higher. This pattern also exists in the corporate world. Management never looks at itself as part of the problem; they only look at the money that they pay to get services done.

As I stated, business is amoral. Rules and regulations are made to be broken, or at least significantly bent. A major NFL coach once said, "A penalty is not a penalty unless you get caught." Well, in business the same is true, so very true.

Business plays the "game of business" so very well. No, this is not a video game, but a philosophy of how things are done in the corporate world. Theory is taught in our education system. The reality of what a business is, well, that is where the rubber meets the road, and it is not pretty. Our noble educators are great on theory but sorely lacking in practicality. The lacking of practicality is by choice, for the real world is much scarier than academia. There was a movie several years ago with a pretty funny comedic actor, Rodney Dangerfield. *Back to School* was the movie. Rodney was in a business class. Listening to a professor explain the inner working of a business, Rodney was not amused. He explained to the professor the reality of what things are really done and why. The professor in turn was not happy.

When the players and refs are commingling, then all bets are off. A case in point: corporate America is in bed with the refs, the government in this case, and so all is fair. Do not get me wrong; physical fornication is not taking place, though sex is a solid asset in business. However, associations are formed and money changes hands. Perception is everything in today's world, and perception does not equate to the truth. When you market something—yourself, an issue, a situation, whatever you want—you put your own "spin" on it so you look like you are the victim, not the source of the problem.

A perception is not necessarily true or factual. It has its basis in fact, but how it is presented, who presents it, and what emphasis is put on certain aspects sway the audience the way the presenter wants. Remember the television ad that appeared years ago stating that "pork is the other white meat"? The lobby for the pork industry was dealing with the red and white meat issue that the government and other health agencies were making in the media that white meats like chicken, turkey, and fish are better for us than the good old hamburger. Well, the pork people were not happy. Pork was getting a bad reputation—not completely wrong, but, still—which led to lower sales and lower profits. Not a good situation for our piggy industry. So the pork industry put a different spin on the situation. Perception was the tool. A pink pork chop, once cooked, was white in color and therefore a "white" meat. Well, it's not a false statement, but it is not true either. It's still red meat—ask your family doctor.

The media is a major force in getting the word out and probably instigating mass hysteria. Who controls the media? Who else but business. Several years ago, a radio personality made a negative comment about the Rutgers women's basketball team. I have heard worse, and maybe it was true and maybe not; however, he was broadcasting out of New York City, adjacent to New Jersey, home of Rutgers. Well, the sponsors got an avalanche of disapproving comments on this. The announcer was fired. Remember this if nothing else: it's always about the money. Some—or should I say many—of these personalities have a tremendous following. What the personality says is taken as gospel. Walter Cronkite had this power when he reported the news on CBS for years. His demeanor, words, presentation, and delivery were second to none. He was quoted the following days on what he said, he was believed, and people followed him. Today, Oprah has that same power.

With regards to IT services, the corporate bean counters have sold the line to management that the cost of computer resources is high and that forecasted costs will be higher. Cost of goods will be higher and profits lower, which is a bad situation for business; this has to be changed, modified, or eliminated to help companies out of this monetary issue. What is a corporation to do? They are taking a hit on earnings and profits. The poor exec can't buy that new yacht or new private jet or keep a mistress in his getaway city. Don't you just feel sorry for the execs? All these are "must-haves" and are needed to keep up with their counterparts.

11: Follow the Yellow Brick Road

No, Dorothy, this is definitely not Kansas. Corporate executives and our elected government officials have made a "utopian environment" for the business community. The United States has this when it comes to IT services. Business has committed a self-inflicted stabbing, a hara-kiri of sorts, with the outsourcing of IT professionals. This significant deficit of IT resources should not be, but is. Business whines about the effects of their self-imposed infliction, cries, or has a hissy fit as if it were a spoiled child. Let's get down to it: business is a spoiled child on steroids. Business always gets rewarded with whatever it wants, whenever it wants it, in my humble opinion, from the yahoos in Washington. Oh, and when I speak of these yahoos, I am not being partisan; the jackass and the elephant, the conservative and the liberal, the Democrats, Republicans, independents, and last but surely not least the tea baggers are all yahoos. Nobody is excluded from Ali Baba and the Forty Thieves, also known as our Congress. Oh yes, 1600 Pennsylvania Avenue is part of this grandiose party as well.

Sometimes, but oh so rarely, our elected puppets throws a "bone" to the masses, but that is only when there is a huge public outcry. Case in point: the credit cards that we all use and of course abuse. Congress put limits on interest and fees imposed by the banking and credit card businesses. The credit card businesses despised this type of reprimand, control, legislation, and government intervention. Retaliation, not mere adherence and compliance, was business's game plan. They attacked the people who wanted this—us, the consumers—by hard-and-fast date limitations, borrowing limitations, and all-around nastiness. And yes, the court jesters in Washington did nothing about that. Need I say more? Meet Bonnie and Clyde, alias Corporate America and Congress.

Then there was the "sequester" issue. The government plays all types of high-level games in trying to get a handle on the national debt and economic issues. In the crosshairs were the air traffic controllers that were furloughed to save money. As a side note, I firmly blame our elected officials, past and present, for this incomprehensible debt we have. Now, back to the "failed" sequester. Furloughing air traffic controllers did not work so well—our elected flunkies did not like the delays at our airports. Why? Very simple: the "all about me" factor. Remember this if nothing else: we, a collective we, only care about ourselves. Charity and "do goodness" only apply when minimal self-sacrifice is needed or when we need to be stroked. Our governmental "essentials" use the airlines as a second home, and when that "apple cart" was disrupted, well, that issue had to be resolved quickly. It's amazing how an issue can be addressed so quickly when its effects are close to home.

There is an additional factor fueling this IT issue: our educators. Yes, the educators of higher learning who spout theory. The same educators who have never worked in the corporate world, who are "book" smart but totally illiterate in "street smarts" in the realm of IT, are guiding the young. Two areas are here: first, what is or is not taught; and, second, the audience who is taking this in.

I will address the audience first. They are the naive, the babes of the world, the uninformed, the students who want and need education and guidance. They readily absorb the rhetoric spewed by the so-called professionals, our teachers, as undeniable doctrine. Students, young and old, hear that information technology is where it's at. They see the ads for educational programs and read the articles touting the "hot" careers, so they assume this is where it at. The IT career is where it is at. But sorry, Charlie; you are a dumb American—no need to apply. Yes, reverse racism, against the hometown American, is played out, excused, and blessed by corporate America. This goes especially to you "do-good liberals" and the non IT people: do not, I repeat do not, say this is not so! It has happened to me. Civil rights laws are not enforced; nothing is done in retaliation, punishment, or retribution. Everything is taken as status quo. These students absorb the bullshit and propagate it at our major companies. The naive student is not at fault here; they follow the adage of Catholics and take it on faith. Most students take the words spouted by professors as being gospel. Pull your pants down, bend over, and grab your ankles; the ride is going to be rough.

The next bone of contention is what or what not is being spewed by the educators. Our college professors oppose teaching our youth COBOL. Why? According to theory—no, forget that; it is plain and simple ignorance. COBOL is supposedly a dead language or technology; it is not the newest and greatest and at best is on life support. Bullshit! As I said previously, practical knowledge of today's corporate world is missing in these pillars of upper education, and the diarrhea of education destroys instead of enhances the minds. Folks, we have to outlaw this propaganda, taught as gospel, by our educators in the same way we treated DDT. DDT was touted as a really good for exterminating insects on our crops, but with many negative side effects on the population it was working for. The same is true of this biased education.

Speaking from the practical and real realm of corporate IT, COBOL is an old language, yes. A cumbersome tool, a wordy language, yes. However, it is a self-documenting language that the non IT person could read and so understand what the code was doing. It is a strong language in some situations and weak in others; as with everything, each job has its proper tool. Retooling, reengineering, or replacing this archaic COBOL has been toyed with for many years, but it has not proceeded past the talking stages. Replacing this language has brought fear to the non-IT world as well as the new IT world. Parallel testing and results arc difficult to ascertain.

There exists an undetermined amount of code that is old but still delivering desired results; it's hard to throw away that old pair of comfy slippers. Change is difficult and costly. Remember the ROI factor and the common statement, "if it ain't broke don't fix it". The business world may want to replace COBOL with something new and improved; however, a justifiable fear is present in corporate management. The cost of this endeavor is just not justified. Getting the same results that they are used to is not guaranteed. The end is not justified by the means. The Y2K issue was known for years but did not get addressed until the eleventh hour. So, as a formable resource that old damn COBOL will stay and stay and stay to eternity.

These same educators that denigrate COBOL also teach new languages. That is good; that is teaching new technology. Change is constant. However, these same educators also poison the minds of those they educate with the doctrine that COBOL is dead and that one's future is doomed if one pursues this path. This statement is perception. It's theory. It's not reality. To be proficient in anything requires its history or its origin or roots as a basis; they should not be discarded as yesterday's news. The educators have done just that.

A parallel to this is Apple. Apple's philosophy on hardware and software revolve around Apple as the center of the IT universe. We all must pay homage to Steve Jobs; not. As the educators poisoned the students' mind so is Apple's dream of being the ultimate in IT. It is not. Apple's products are not widely accepted by the business world. Why? The reason is very obvious to IT folks: it does not play well with non-Apple hardware or software. Apple diehards will challenge this statement, but I have seen this play out in several of my last assignments. The non-Apple hardware makes universalized storage, communications, connections, and wiring so that hardware made by company A may be connected to another piece of hardware manufactured by company B; for example, a Dell PC can be connected to a Hewlett-Packard printer. As I stated previously about commandments of the business: business does not care about it competitors, only itself. Yes this true, as usual there are exceptions and this is one of them. Playing nice with competitors or associated companies is good for all parties involved.

Our educators, in my opinion, are as stupid as the theory they teach. I am not saying that they are illiterates, but they are not in touch with reality. A decent analogy to this is so-called "reality" television. It's all scripted for the rating gods; it is not real. Technology is growing, and they are on the cutting edge in teaching it. Fine. But the old is still there and will stay there as long as there is no viable solution with an acceptable ROI. I have been in the business for over thirty years and have seen and done many things. The biggest fear or obstacle of the profession is keeping up with technology. Technology grows like shade-grown tobacco on a hot, humid day: fast. Keeping up with technology is a never-ending battle; new kinds of code or languages, new types of databases, new communications to programmers or customers or devices or networks and platforms, to name a few factors of the business.

Once IT was introduced, IT became a vital and permanent asset in conducting business. No matter the language, database, or technology, business has passed the point of no turning back. The line of demarcation has been reached. IT has crossed it. Bid welcome to your new houseguest.

A constant, crossing over all IT, as it was in the beginning and will be into the future, will be logic. Logic is needed in all phases of IT: how one accomplishes something, the steps, the results, and dealing with the outcome of what happen. So no matter the coded language a computer technician uses to communicate with this mysterious box of electronics, the logic of going from A to B will always exist.

This behavior by the educators has tinkered with a vital law in the world of economics, the law of supply and demand. The higher the supply the lower the demand, which plays into lower salaries; therefore, why go in debt to your eyeballs when you will not have a chance of earning the dollars to pay this debt back? Conversely this same economic rule of supply and demand has increase the value of an American IT resource. Why? One, COBOL is not going away. Two, new American IT resources that know COBOL are not being produced. Three, the old American IT resource, who was outsourced; he either found a new career, retired, or expired, matriculated, died. And four, the outsource candidates cannot do the job that is in the same quality as the Americans did. As I have stated, IT work within a company has no enemy. The work needed in the IT departments of our businesses constantly grows. Once IT was added to the business model, there was no turning back. Business and IT have been joined at the hip as Siamese twins; business needs IT for all it does, and the business will fail if IT does not exist. So, teach what you want, but realty dictates what is really needed.

I have a financial advisor; everybody should have a trusted soul to help them maneuver through the jungle of investing and savings. Several years ago, when we were reviewing our financial game plan, he said that we should have some money in emerging markets. Growth and investments were great; returns were great, so invest. Also at that same time, several colleagues were recruited to teach COBOL in *India*. The hourly rates were very generous. Things were not all positive; the positions required extended stays in India, compound living, and dealing with climate issues. Also, language and logistics were an issue. Many of us know our business, but teaching on a formal level is different. Yes, we have trained and mentored on a one-to-one basis, but this was different. None of us had the foresight or intuition to realize that this was beginning of our careers' demise. These same emerging markets, touted as a great investment, were producing our replacements. So IT, unknowingly worked on its own demise by training these third world replacements. Also to take a share of the blame is everybody. That sounds harsh, please hear me out. I am not saying that the investing was covert, vindictive, or greed. This investment in emerging markets was touted as a good thing for our portfolios, so we follow our financial people's advice. Maybe we should read those ultra-boring prospectuses, they print them, but really who reads them. I take responsibility for my investing prowess, I did invest. As the title states IT'S ALWAYS ABOUT THE MONEY, and so it is.

Now that the wolf in sheep's clothing had reared his evil head, companies simultaneously downsized while lobbying for more H1B1 visas, claiming that technical resources were not available. Artificially, this was true. The new class of computer science majors had very little or no COBOL. Business freed themselves from their own competent American IT staffs by attrition and layoffs. So yes, there was a deficiency, but it was a self-imposed deficiency. Then, just as if it were planned—and I know it was—the foreign firms stepped in, stating that they could supply needed services offshore in their countries at a fraction of American rates while providing the same quality. And the crack in the door opened, and the flood-waters rushed in. The true product of the "emerging markets", foreign IT personnel has inundated on American businesses.

American companies bought this. In fact, they bred this, they nurtured it, they loved it, they planned and perpetrated it, and they propagated it. Why would American companies work to get rid of the American IT work force? Don't forget, oh little wee one, the business always comes first. In conjunction with IT services being numero uno, IT represents costs which are more important to the business. Businesses courted their new, exotic, and intimate bed partners by stating that they had a need for IT talent but that our schools were not producing them. This was true and false at the same time. Our educators were biasing students by scaring them away from languages and skills that were not, in fact, going away. These old languages were taught to offshore resources, and those resources walked right in.

Another issue was unearthed like a zombie apocalypse. This was an issue that affected not only our technological students but all students contemplating post-graduate studies. Why go massively in debt in order get an advance degree and then not find employment in the corporate sector to balance the scales? I am not saying students were entitled to employment because they went to school, but all sorts of positions were given away wholesale to foreign counterparts. Why? Simple: corporate management does what corporate management wants. Business has made inroads with the third-world nations to bring back indentured servitude, a feudal practice in earlier times in Europe. Is this history or déjà vu?

Business cut most if not all ties with their local IT talent by bringing in foreign talent on the premise that the foreign talent offered better resources at a lower cost. With the floodgates open to the so-called supreme IT talent, American corporations have propagated and nurtured these substandard resources. I have seen American management kiss the brown asses of these rejects biblically, philosophically, and figuratively. I have been a vendor or IT consultant for most of my career. As an outside resource you are a hired gun. You are not a person. You are brought in to take orders and perform. You are not to change management. You are not to do as you see fit or to follow your own personal agenda. You are told where to do your work, who to report to, and when. However, I have seen many of these golden children of IT get their way on projects with American management, reestablishing the Wild West, only this time in IT. This proves my point and eliminates any doubt that current business management has no blessed idea about what they are doing with regards to IT and technological services. The really scary point here is they, management, think they are doing a great job. Houston, we have a problem here.

The current class of management has regained the previously thought lost control over IT. The cost of IT within corporations has theoretically dropped dramatically, and that makes earnings look great. *Cost*, though, is a very nebulous term. From what I've observed, current IT work is not a pretty picture. Time-tested procedural IT tasks are not being performed. Work-arounds are the standard, and the do-over coefficient is at an all-time high. However, the biggest and least reported benefit to the IT business was the repeal of the abolishment of slavery. President Lincoln, your proclamation has been repealed. Slavery is alive and flourishing in corporate America today! I can only presume the war in the 1860s known as the Civil War can go down in the annals of history as a loss, a loss next to the Vietnam and Middle East fiascos. Management has exploited this newfound pool of resources, having them jumping through hoops and working all kinds of hours—while, by the way, not getting additional pay. This foreign contingency of nomads travel throughout the country, without the benefits of reimbursed expenses, work fifteen-plus hour days, and accept this with no questions asked. Why do these resources do this? Simple: they get out of their hellholes, their homelands. Many of them migrate here with families and expect their sexist and class morals to exist here.

12: Why?

We are all creatures of habit. When we do something once and it all goes well, we then assume we should continue doing it, embarking on a journey down the yellow brick road. Tradition, supposedly a "golden rule" passed down from our parents, carries a lot of weight in our minds. Tradition mimics habits. We are taught or inbred with a predisposition and follow it as imprinted ducklings follow a toy. Do we ever question tradition? Is there a better wheel? Do we assume the past is the only path for the future? Are we as dumb as sheep headed to the slaughterhouse? Yes, as I have said, I am a student of history. So we follow the yellow brick road to hell. However, we have seen the destruction of tradition and habits; could history be that warning beacon? Is tradition the only path?

Reengineering is a scary and foreboding term, but what is reengineering? This term is or was part of IT systems vernacular several years back. It refers to reexamining a process, a system, a way things are being done. Can we make a better wheel? An ominous questioning about an object that has been around since fire and water; however, in the world of systems, the question does have credence. Technology advancements, outdated and unwarranted processes, and new processes are but a glimmer of what is going on in our world. Systems need to keep up. Yes, Virginia, a better wheel is possible.

When we examine our own life's path, the trials and tribulations of our ancestors, the way they were, do we accept it as tradition, or do we look for a better wheel? A couple or individual has a child; that's nice. It is common for parents and guardians to say they want to give this new life a better set of life's experiences than what the parents had. Now I am not saying that the parents have migrated from hell, but things can always be improved on. Life is tough and sprinkled with a myriad of obstacles. Is it accepted that the man screws other men to gain top dog status, or do we resist? Tradition is neither always correct nor always wrong; rather, it provides guidance to the audience. Yes, business would like to maintain the status quo; it's cost effective, and we all know businesses' attitude to the almighty dollar—it's their *god*. Business is always looking at and trying to reevaluate the business equation in their favor. There will be casualties in this economic war. So I say attack this foe. Capitalism is great, but it must be tempered with realism and foresight.

Why do I unequivocally hate the concept of a global economy? I do not deny the existence of such a philosophy that extends far beyond our physical boundaries. However, there are inherent and unseen meanings that we, the totally naive populace, is shielded from.

When we say "global economy" we imply an equal and level playing field. Let's consider a football game. There are eleven players on each team on field at one time, the field of play is one hundred yards long, and the goalposts are always at the end of the end zone. Wherever the game is played, these are given facts, and so equality is achieved.

Now consider economics. No, this is not a diatribe about the dollar versus the euro, just simple, everyday behavior. We go to our local grocer and buy food. There are many grocers, and our preference is purely subjective, but the behavior is the same: we pay money for product. I am not going into product quality, which is subjective on so many levels. You need food to survive, and one person may want the 70 percent hamburger while another chooses the 90 percent. All I am saying is that an exchange is made to satisfy both parties, money for food.

Here is where I get my point across. Corporate America has said so many times that the product—IT services provided by the foreign market—is equal to if not better than the domestic product. This is the battle between the 70 percent and 90 percent products. Well, this is not true and is my basis for arguing against the global economy philosophy. Here are my documented facts:

- The sources of these resources are far behind what we have locally. There is a valid reason for them to be called third world. The United States has far superior technologies from tools to manpower.

- We are giving our economy away as if it were a fire sale, but why? Are we getting something better in return? I remember working on Y2K where a foreign firm came in to do a significant amount of the work. The justification by management was that we would later sell more products to them. This did not happen.

- Technology is not like any other product. This product builds upon itself. This chain must not be broken, or else the growth stagnates. Technology is in the present, but even more so it is the way of the future. The future of our lives is in the infinity and beyond. We must sustain and nurture this natural resource. IT's worth far surpasses the gold rendered to Caesar.

- There is no equality in the commonality of the IT resource. Yes, we are all men and women in the biological and biblical senses. But that's all she wrote. Technology has no equal partner away from our shores.

- The concept of equality is but a myth. Nations strive to equal us. America is the gold standard. Business is not in the charity business. Business is in an economic war.

The global economy is not and never will be a level playing field. It sure sounds non-Christian, and maybe it is, but reality has spoken. The economy is slanted in favor of the haves and not the "have nots". Okay, Christians, get your stones out ready to slam me, but this is true. We care about ourselves first; others will be satisfied later. However, we will and do exploit the "have nots" for our own personal gains. We will do this and dress it up to appease the press. So, based on the pretense of global economy, we bring the masses in.

Superiority reigns now as it will always. Corporate executives claim that the global economy allows them to obtain services of equal quality with the benefit of lower cost providing the operative advantage. In reality, however, the foreign IT resource is so far behind the American resource it is not even on the same planet. Technology has always been in our backyard. It's like basketball; we are the dream team. This is not bravado and me banging my chest as a defiant gorilla. It is a bona fide, pure, and simple fact like 1 + 1 = 2. So the replacement of resources with an inferior IT skills is corporate destruction, plain and simple.

Yes, this sounds bitter. Yes, this is very contradictory to the verbiage spouted by the government and corporate bigwigs, but it is oh so very true. I do have a single question to those who defend outsourcing: have you had the opportunity to work with these substandard technicians? Talk with them? Deal with their own selfish needs? I have seen it. I have worked with them. And I have suffered at the hands of these golden children of IT. In their defense, they make great Slurpees, but that is it.

Yes! Yes! Yes, to that war cry: life is unfair! We have all seen and heard the "war" stories of what our parents endured during their lives. I presume we accepted this as a rite of passage for our own lives, the basis of tradition. However, in the same vein, our parents have said on many occasion that "they would like to make their kids' lives better than what they had. We have seen health care, technological advancements, and education to name a few that have improved over time. Yes, a better wheel is attainable. The

Catholic religion says "take it on faith" when they cannot or do not want to answer a question. In the past this was acceptable, today we do not. Is this wrong? Everything should not be freely accepted, especially the questionable and oppressive activities, and chalk it up to tradition. Bullshit! There are circumstances, and outsourcing is one of them, that can and should be addressed head-on and not lying down. The Neolithic times, some 6500-4500 BC, saw the origin of our wheel; at that time is was a major find and the establishment of ground zero. I presume this 'wheel' is the starting line to find, create, build, or discover something better. I have said this in the past with regards to records. Records are made to be broken. So here we go.

13: Hocus, Pocus … Voila

Most of us enjoy the performance of an accomplished magician, his illusions, sleight of hand, disappearing objects, or the levitation of objects. Fantasy takes hold of reality, if only for a moment. We, the totally baffled audience, try to determine the all-important question: how did he do that? Corporate America has become David Copperfield. Not as dramatic or show-stopping as Houdini but just as spellbinding and awe-inspiring as a Las Vegas show.

The economic principle of supply and demand is manipulated by the law of numbers as performed by our corporate executives. Numbers can tell many if not all stories, in many different ways. Numbers can be manipulated the old-fashioned way—just change them, the old "fudge-factor" approach—or they can be presented in such a way to show what a person or other entity wants the audience to see. It is the perception principal played to the fullest.

Businesses played along with the educators and their bullshit line that old technology like COBOL is dead and not worth the time to study; there is no life in it. Do not forget corporate management is the next step for our college-misinformed graduates, a place where they can propagate what they were taught. Remember, current business management really has no practical IT exposure and are so gullible. Let's forget about the PC version; current IT management and business management would fuck up a wet dream, and they are stupid to the *n*th degree. Many students of technology, naive students, fell prey to the educated elite and avoided these COBOL classes, as they were deemed "doomed" technologies. Contrary to the educators' theoretical knowledge of the real world, their so-called expertise, there was, is, and will be a tremendous demand for these archaic skills like COBOL, and the foreign areas knew this.

Business was playing a shrewd game of poker, not showing their hand as they rid themselves of highly qualified American resources, by playing along with the educators' lectures. Why not? They themselves are the product of such bullshit. Corporations were executing a common tactic in poker, the bluff. The bluff, in lay-men's terms, is a lie; however, you sell this lie with positive force. In poker, when you have a lousy hand, a, sure loser, after you have sized up your opponents, you may decide to lie to them. With that in mind you bet, heavily and with force, in order to convey that you are confident your cards are powerful enough to win the pres-ent hand. The other players must, at a minimum, match the bet and better yet bump their bets to show superiority. The opponents may have better hand, but are they willing to put up or will they just shut up? If the opponents fold, the bluff wins. In poker, to see your opponents' cards, you must match the highest bet. If no bet is made, then the cards are not seen and the question of whether or not a player was bluffing is left unanswered on the table. What this boils down to is that the corporate sector is a fraternity of liars.

Students were victims of the bluff as played out by the theory-based educators; they revised their studies and avoided the technology. Our education structure changed to reflect the lower or non-ex-isting demand for these skills and stopped producing skilled re-sources. Business saw their partners, the educators, and their phi-losophy and played right along. Corporate executives had their game plan to regain the lost control of IT.

Business is a happy camper: there are no new local resources; step 1 was EOJ with COND CODE 0000 (for those who are not IT, this translates to "good job"). Business still had another issue, however: the current IT department. These departments had older, extremely skilled, and talented technicians and other highly compensated resources that the business area wanted to replace.

Previously stated in the ten commandments of a business, is that the business is a dynamic and living entity or organism constantly changing for the betterment of itself. Business will do whatever it takes for its own good and will use any and all means to achieve it. And so it did: it "downsized", learning to do more with less. This is a partial truth. This was a means to "clean house" and reestablish the IT department with a controllable resource consisting of third-world, substandard but subservient technicians. IT business continued, but older resources were too costly and were not playing well with the illiterate and misinformed corporate management, so they had to go. They had to train their replacements, and then vanished into obscurity. This is the gospel according to corporations about the world of IT.

As I said, the work in IT never stops. It constantly grows, needing neither sunlight nor water; only the business nurtures it. However the amount of IT work is not a straight line nor cumulative of the past. The amount of work, at a point in time, does vary; sometimes more and sometimes less. This is a function solely of the business. The number of IT resources varies proportionally to the workload at hand. Seeing additional IT resources from vendors or independent sources periodically is nothing new. This was the start of the foreign influence; the Middle East, Asia, and Europe all supplied IT resources. The American IT worker saw this and really was not affected one way or another; it was corporate management's decision, and IT work had to be done. Step 2 was the beginning of the corporate game plan, the downsizing of their present IT staffs. Corporate America was introducing themselves to the outside world of resources and began purging the costly American IT resource. Step 2 is not yet at EOJ; however, a major percentage of this step is done, and the results, at least according to corporate bean counters, look good.

The removal of qualified American resources, either by attrition, layoffs, or downsizing, basically created a false environment was created in the IT departments of American business. New domestic talent training was nearly stopped or severely curtailed, but the demand for their services is always there. Welcome the golden children of IT to save the day. Yes, corporate executives got their wishes, but as it has been said, be careful what you wish for, because you just might get it. There it was, the mother lode of cheap resources, just there for the picking. It was like Eve enticing Adam with that damn apple. Now there was just one thing: the leaders in Washington have laws about how many foreigners we let in to get American jobs. Let's go back to the commandments. Whenever there's a law on the books, adapt it to the business's interest. Yes, there is an X-rated, intimate affair between corporate leaders and our government. Yes, their very unholy alliance needed to rob Peter to pay Paul, and that is what business did to open the floodgates holding back cheap, incompetent resources. As I said, business takes no prisoners; everybody is expendable.

14: Oh What a Tangled Web We Weave, When First We Practice to Deceive

Perception, according to Webster, is the result of perceiving, and to perceive is to attain awareness or understanding of an idea, issue, or problem. Perception is the tool or mechanism used to sell an idea, principal, or ideology. Perception is used by one and all; nobody is beyond reproach on using this device to persuade others to accept a favorable or wanted opinion. After all, we want it our way. Perception, even though it has it basis in the truth, does not equate to truth. Selling a perception is selling a view of the issue at hand for the seller's benefit. For example, a pharmaceutical company is advertising some kind of medication to eliminate pain. Evidence to support this will be shown, evidence that may even degrade the competition's product. Is this correct? Were things said, omitted, or shown in such a way to put a favorable light on the seller's product? Yes. Lying is not exactly done here; the more acceptable verbiage is telling "their version of the truth".

Business, or should I say the corporate elite, use perception to sway any and all to get what they ultimately want. As I have stated and substantiated previously, business has a love-hate relationship with their IT departments; thus, business has an internal problem. Businesses do not like problems. Problems equate to business costs. Businesses solve problems to their advantage. Lest we forget, the business is number one at all costs, and all other factors are expendable.

Now that business had bought into the educators' theory about "old" technology and that their present IT departments needed attention, what were they going to do? Simply stated, business will always need IT resources. This hard-and-fast truth will only change when the computer, as we know it, is in the Smithsonian. This is not going to happen in our lifetime. Back to the IT resources, they had to be monetarily cheap, they had to be totally at the mercy of business, and there had to be a never ending supply of them. The answer, of course, was outsourcing. Welcome, yes welcome the golden children of IT, to the land of corporate America.

Businesses makes awkward bedfellows, at least when it suits itself. Let me explain this phenomenon. The NFL has a loyal following; most fans have an almost religious allegiance to their team. I have been a New York Giant fan for over fifty years; I bleed Giant blue, and I stoically follow and watch my team. No, I do not have any financial or any other ties to the Giants; however, it is my team. This same philosophy is shared by most fans. On any given day during league play, I always watch. However, at a point in time I will sometimes cheer on a dreaded rival of my team, such as the Dallas Cowboys. Why? Very simple: if by the Cowboys winning would help my Giants, then it's a no-brainer. Confusing, treason-like, or just plain wrong, for some it's a hard concept to grasp. My wife thinks I am crazy, but all fans know and do this in support of their team.

Back to business. Business categorically despises the government with all its taxes, rules, and regulations. However, there are times deeper intimacy is needed, and this was one of them. Businesses complained about the lack of local technical talent. Yes, this problem was self-inflicted and artificially created, but it was means to an end. The corporate sector was the problem; however, corporate management never allowed itself to be blamed as the cause of the problem. Remember, the business is always right. In the business's eyes, the world revolves around it. So here we have introduced and fortified the "foreign IT" resource issue and need. Government imposes limitations on these resources for many reasons, but common sense and reasonability are discarded like yesterday's newspaper when business supplies a significant amount of dead presidents to our elected officials. Ah yes, the most famous misnomer of all times, *common sense*—especially when it comes to our elected. Like a new tax that is passed by these same turkeys as a temporary measure, the floodgates were opened and unlikely to be closed.

Once this ruse was started, business had to continue to propagate this story—better yet, lie about it. After all, it was a win-win for business: cheap labor and outright control. The game plan was to keep it going and expand it, and so they did with more deceptions—whoops, I mean perceptions. Corporate leaders proceeded by hounding the government; actually, it was more like whining the way a child does in a store to get that needed plastic object, the toy. Our flunkies on Capitol Hill heard a barrage of statements and forecasts by business. These statements professed doom and gloom in the business world because the IT expertise needed for their businesses was not available. It was a true statement, however artificially created the situation was. The IT talent had been here yesterday but was gone today. That was true since our education system had stopped producing them and further perpetrated by corporations eliminating their IT staffs by downsizing. Yes, a lie was created and propagated. Doesn't this look eerily like the so-called gasoline shortage of the 1970s, which had been artificially created to jack up profits?

The powers that be, our pseudo-statesmen, seeing a perceived issue, kept increasing the number of H1B1 visas in order to allow more and more foreign IT resources in. This was good for a start, but the perception that was next promoted was even more outlandish— these foreign technical gurus, from depressed third-world nations, were touted and acclaimed as the next coming of Christ in the land of IT. Yep, Jesus Christ himself came back to earth in the form of a techie. Interesting analogy; however, let us keep going. This was one of the biggest lies perpetrated. I, as an American technical IT resource, take resounding issue with this *lie*. Have they, corporate executives, worked with these substandard IT resources, tried to communicate with them, even just coexisted with them? No, they have not. Plain and simple, they are flunkies, pure, unadulterated rejects, not the second coming of Christ for the technology age. We as Americans defined, created, and built the technology machine. It was not lost to any foreign entity.

The story is evolving like a cancerous tumor. I must persevere; the topic is near and dear to me, my friends, my country, everything. You, the reader, might say that you are retired, so why should you care? I guess that is one view. However, my take on this is that this bullshit of the "global economy" and outsourcing is not in the past as was WWII or landing on the moon. It is a work in progress. Today, I saw an article on HLN about the "happiest place on earth", well, at least according to Disney. They are eliminating American workers and replacing them with the Indian variety. They—that is, Disney—said the American can keep their positions a little longer if they train their replacements. Isn't this great, getting canned with compassion? Disney, take your cross-dressing rodent and stick it where the sun don't shine! Folks, this not new, this is not "shock journalism" or "shock and awe"; this is real. I have seen this same scenario played in front of my own eyes and ears. Yep, fine corporate establishments that I have worked at did exactly that to my colleagues and friends. This explains my non-PC attitude, bitterness, my reasoning for writing this. This is the same story with different players. It is being played out everywhere and will be played out places yet to be determined.

So there you are; you are going to be hanged. Here is the rope; make your own noose. The intent of the H1B1 visa was not to remove and replace American workers. It was to create another temporary source to supplement American IT staff. As we all know, corporate management will create any advantage it can and take every possible advantage of any existing situation with no regards to the carnage or aftermath. So, as with the 401(k), we have total abuse of the H1B1. However, I do take solace in the fact that the war is not over, just the skirmish at hand.

Again, I make no apology for my outspoken, crude, crass, and racist words. This is not a PC topic; it is war. I am a boater, and when I take my craft out I am in charge, totally. It's not a democracy but a dictatorship. Yes, a dictatorship authorized by the Coast Guard. As a captain or person at the helm, I am responsible for my actions, the boat's actions, and the actions of any passengers on my boat. The penalties are stiff and lethal. Any infraction by those listed will be charged to me for retribution. So when I say something on that boat, it's the gospel. I feel the same about what I'm saying here about this outsourcing issue.

Being part of a proud community of IT professionals and seeing this propagation of pure shit being taken as gospel, well, this totally burned my ass. A lie was sold to our government jokers, and that government actually bought it; this has more than branded my mind. Business and government were and still are in bed with each other, and the populace who voted these jokers in, to put it succinctly, got "greeked". Business had finally achieved what it always wanted: total control of IT without knowing a blessed thing. And they say knowledge is power. Think about it. Folks, this is an accurate and disturbing picture of what and how perception is used. Yes, little ones, this is but only one example of the devious effects of perception.

15: Codices Simian

Circle this day on your calendar as if it were 9/11 or the day Kennedy was assassinated; the aftermath of this finding will have the same dismal effects on us and our economy. Liberals will stand in horror and disbelief; business in its typical fashion will deny, deny, deny; and the illiterate non-techie will be amazed. Those of us who are "in the business", however, will nod our heads and applaud for the release of this fact. For today is the day the Codices Simian will finally be formally documented. Until now it was a dirty little innuendo made by IT professionals as to the wishes and aspirations of corporate management. Julian Assange and Edward Snowden were not the only ones to release dirty little secrets; I too will expose the dialogue long said in the hallowed halls of our IT departments. Now the "mystical ghost" is outed and has a physical component. No, it is not like the birth of a child. This is, at least in my opinion, the first time that someone has documented this parasite openly. The ruse, perception, and lies created by corporate greed, inspired and fortified by the government, have spawned a new being. An *Alien,* from another land, planet, or universe has set up roots on American soil. Under the auspices of capitalism, this gave the corporate mongers the green flag to perpetrate a monumental crime of the century on America, surpassing Bernie Madoff's insatiable greed and deception.

This new species will not be documented or proclaimed by any members of the scientific community. Again this species will not be acknowledged in any of the world-class journals of the science, and as a matter of fact it will probably go totally unnoticed other than this book. On the other hand, I will be labeled a racist and advocate of ethnic warfare, and I will, basically, be blasted again for exposing corporate America's dirty little secret. This writing will be called bullshit. The liberals and the non-IT out there will refuse to believe it. Yes, I will be slammed, to say the least, for writing this. But the exposure of this will be at the very least disturbing to the guilty or the corporate sector. However the IT professional has talked about this wish of business, in private and unbeknownst of corporate management for many years. Corporate executives wanted the "Codices Simian", and they finally got them. As the proverb states, be careful for what you wish for—you just might get it; corporate America finally got its wish. Merry Christmas and do have a Happy Holidays.

In a scientific fashion, document, photograph, understand, and study the phenomena. A new species has been discovered! Call the biologists. Call the natural scientists. Call the doctors. And yes, do not forget to call *National Geographic*; they have great photographers. This is a new find or a mutation can be found posing as an IT resource on the campuses of our corporations. This species is totally new to America, appearing for the first time on American soil. What is this? Who is this? What is the origin? Is it friend or foe? What are the ramifications? Should we as Americans be afraid? All are valid questions that will be explored in next several passages.

Let me say this about me: I do not lie. I am not PC, so if I offend the meek and naive, so sorry; go take a hike off a short pier. Being that I am a student of technology, the written word in my world is always black and white—no fifty shades of gray here. I have encountered people who have not had the opportunity to see or experience what I have firsthand. They—the blind, the so naive, or the corporate puppets—do have a hard time fathoming this fact, but they do come around. I am a proponent of capitalism and a realist. So you liberal "do-gooders", go fuck yourself, and smell the coffee. Everybody is aboard the *Titanic*, and yes, we are taking on water, very cold water!

Now back to the Codices Simian. Common man will see them, react to them, converse with them, work with them, and even be social with them. However, the common man can't see the forest for the trees. He is oblivious to what is there in front of his eyes. This writing will be considered racist or unflattering to the ethnicity, but it is true; they are here. Where did they come from? This is simple, oh grasshopper; they have been spawned or developed by the corporate sector, they are what corporate management wanted. Businesses always get what they want; do not forget business is amoral and rules are made to be broken—or should I say stretched to the extreme. As a footnote, Spanx will not help hiding those stretch marks,

Corporations need IT for the obvious reasons stated previously. However, control over the technology resources by the non-technical among us has been perceived to be out of reach, until now. The business hierarchy has been leveled, at least in management's eyes, to the way it was before those damn computers. This was written about years ago in a journal about the technical side of business; in short, it stated that current IT personnel should be aware that their next boss would not have IT knowledge or experience. This is abundantly true; I have seen, interviewed, and worked for such incompetent people, and the experience rivaled getting a root canal. However, the most frightening aspect of the explosion of non-technical IT management, at least in my eyes, is that they think they are so very qualified because of some half-assed classes in Project Management, no practical just words. Alexander Pope's statement that "a little learning is a dangerous thing" has come to life in the age of technology.

From the corporate point of view, there is one and only one thing, and that is the total control of the masses. Management has regained the power and control, has total autonomy to make all decisions regarding anything in business, now that technology has become one of their loyal subjects. A simple analogy regarding this concept would be giving a senior citizen, who is used to driving an automobile, he lovingly calls a "four-banger", an upgrade to a Ferrari. Heaven help us. The current batch of management has no idea or concept of what IT is and therefore does not know how to manage it, but they have control, full control. Not knowing technology is only part of this business equation; people are the other part. The American IT professional is competent, is paid well, communicates with all needed resources, and is a major asset for a corporation. The IT professional will not be bullied, coerced, or convinced to do things through threats or without being treated fairly. I traveled significantly during my IT tenure, and the clients that utilized my services paid the agreed-upon rate and expenses; this was the norm for all my peers. The new foreign IT resources, if you can call the technologically inept a resource, just migrate as nomads in the desert to wherever they are sent, with no allegiances or loyalties; they just aimlessly do it. The codices simian work, if you can call what they do work, unacceptably long hours, with no stipend for expenses; this is the new norm, and corporate management takes more than full advantages of this. It sounds depressing to the American IT resource, and it most certainly is. The codices simian are coddled and given a plethora verbal attributes, constantly "stroked", never challenged about what they do or do not do, and revered as almost a god to IT. I called this the spoiled baby syndrome. Classism, sexism, their own nationalism, and just plain incompetence are what they really bring to the table. That is the bottom line. Corporate management loves this. Lincoln may have freed one set of slaves, but slavery is alive and kicking and in full bloom as we speak. The corporate sector is the old-fashioned cotton plantation owner brought to the twenty-first century on steroids.

I have documented the genealogy of the codices simian (for those who do not know the scientific vernacular, it's the code monkey). For any person to call another person a monkey is pretty horrific, I agree. However, in conversations with corporate management, at all levels, this was the bottom line. Corporate executives, in not so many words, asked for the code monkey. They described what they wanted, chastised the American IT resource they have, and created a "new" subservient IT resource. Bottom line, corporations got what they wished for.

Present management wanted control, total control, and they have achieved nirvana. Management has taken several cursory IT courses, assigned work and abilities to an arbitrary matrix, aligned corporate management on the almighty dollar, and slam, bam, presto, we have the code monkey.

American corporate management has observed the IT professional in his work, education, and performance and equated that to what this supposedly superior resource has to offer. The code monkey's skills are said to parallel if not exceed those of the American IT resource. He is theoretically proclaimed to be better educated. Let me expound here for a moment. Better educated? An interesting question. If so, then why as an American IT resource have I, along with all other resources, been asked to prove our upper education at the technical and college level? I am not comparing educational systems, however the statement has been made by the corporate sector that they are better educated. I definitely disagree with that statement. In the early days of IT, all resources were trained. The training could have been formal and some by fire. Hands on as I like to put it. Today I presume that they want a more formal approach. Could there be a more sinister reason in asking to prove your education? Shall we say fraud? Could corporate management have had an epiphany and seen the light? These subjective qualities of which I speak are unadulterated bullshit. The real reason is cost and control—no, it is slavery by management.

Non-technical management observed the old IT professional, yes, the Americans. Corporate executives feared the unknown and the powerful, even though they worked side by side with them. What they took back from their so-called exhaustive but inconclusive study was: the IT career was easy, staff was arrogant, and unwarranted tasks were done that did not need or have to be done or in other words paid for. This new species is totally and unequivocally subservient to present management; it will kiss corporate management's collective asses, and in turn corporate management will not chastise them and instead will back their actions no matter what. The spoiled code monkey is thriving on American soil. Ortho, have we got something to control this pest?

Business's presentation of and accolades for the code monkey are filled with glowing reviews, as if a new gold mine has been found. Corporate executives will say the follow with regards to this new species:

- He is superior to the American IT resource. In reality he is not. I have seen Americans train and mentor this alien resource.

- He costs less than the native IT resource. Yes, no, maybe. On-site he receives relatively the same rate, so it's a wash there. His abilities are suspect, and tasks are constantly being redone, so no savings here. Offshore, well, when you pay a dollar per hour, you get what you pay for.

- Better worker, no slave.

- Better educated, yes if you consider making a Slurpee a viable profession

The truth is actually different.

- Business will never formally admit to this for the obvious; however, they have resurrected slavery. No, Mr. Lincoln, you did end slavery. American business management expects hours of services to be performed but not compensated for. There are several thoughts on this. First and foremost; the American resource would not do this, at least not for extended periods of time. Just because the code monkey is on foreign land, does not equate him to being substandard in his eyes and his fellow monkeys. He tolerates what we consider bad working conditions, why? His homeland is worst. He has acquired some American traits. One of which is making a name for himself. Yes he wants that. Permanent new home. He has compared the two and prefers ours. However the big question is this. What is his internal game plan? The old question where do you want to be in five years? The more we are different, the more we are the same.

- Their communication skills are atrocious. No, that is too high of an accolade. The code monkey is totally non-understandable or coherent. Language, business, business product knowledge, knowledge into American life styles and mores do not exist. I see a massive contradiction here. In all the requirements presented to me, communication is high on the requirements. Have I missed the boat? Do we as Americans, need Rosetta Stone classes to learn additional languages so that we can communicate at our positions here in the States?

- Business has control. They were always in control by the mere fact that they had the checkbook. They are lord and master. With outsourcing, corporate America has reverted to a feudal state. The monarchy of Henry the VIII has re-emerged—off with your head, you peasant.

- The code monkey's mores, customs, practices, and other homeland traits are brought forward and supersede the American way of life. This is a definite factor, one disintegrating our heritage.

As a recap, these non-American IT resources, with limited skills, with questionable communications, who believe in the sexism and classism of their homeland but give the American management full control, have won a place in corporate Disneyland. Heaven help all of us.

16: Coulda, Woulda, Shoulda

Hindsight is always twenty-twenty, so clear and so vivid; if only we could have had it to pick those winning lottery numbers. Were we, the tech-savvy resources, so blinded by the light? Were we so gullible, so naive to believe and trust corporate management? Were we wrong to be so trusting of the inhabitants Capitol Hill, our so-called leaders?

Good technical resources know their position: the here and now, what needs to be done, and when the implementation is to be. This is the mantra of the IT resources by which we constantly live and die. Many of us, however, were oblivious to what was happening in the outside world as it affected IT. The management world of corporations and the movement of IT resources from third-world nations to the United States were not even blips on our radar. In the universe of IT, bringing in vendors, consultants, or American companies to run or assist on IT projects is nothing new. To see any number of IT vendors was and is commonplace; it happens all the time to increase staff for a period of time and then release them. This is the nature of the beast. This is IT work.

The only and most pertinent concerns of most IT professionals, once they are in the business, are keeping up with technology and focusing on a niche that interests them. Education in IT languages, databases, new technologies, new hardware, and software advances are always in the viewfinder and on the mind of an IT resource. The "IT environment" is so very large no single person has a meaningful grasp of all the aspects of IT. Finding a niche that the IT professional excels in is a good thing. The constant training and tweaking of those skills is nothing new. The IT resource is constantly in learning and training mode. This is not a "nice to have" but a matter of survival.

Change is a constant factor in both the corporate and IT worlds. How something is done, what is needed, where to do it, and who is the best resource are always in flux and to be determined. Both entities are very dynamic; thus, change is always on the horizon. Everything and everyone is in play, and the bottom line is the only objective. Corporations do not work via a knee-jerk response; instead they do work slowly and methodically at all times, but movement is constant. The "IT workforce" is a dynamic entity. Resources are getting old, and therefore replacement is normal. Attrition through retirement or changing companies does happen and will continue to add the dynamism of the corporate sector. The replacement of resources is a common practice, but with whom is the issue. Americans, in the past, were replaced with other Americans; it was all in the family. Unbeknownst to the locals, the total American technical resources pool was receiving an infusion of foreign tech firms. It might not have been discussed in the customary sales pitch, but in reality they were putting down a solid foundation in our corporate world. The real intentions of corporate management—to use their new find of supposedly tech savvy and so-called superior IT resources to replace American techies—was not readily apparent or obvious to us. Corporate executives had begun lining their ducks in a row for what they wanted: to resume total control of business and to eliminate IT management.

The "IT project" is always in the crosshairs of corporate management. The planning is an obsession and the execution a nightmare. Incomplete specifications, signoff, personal agendas, numerous and almost ridiculous procedures, and the ever-present politics are the main obstacles, not the IT tasks at hand. IT management, on the other hand, is much more structured: planning, coding, testing, contingencies, and implementation procedures are the basis for a successful implementation. IT, being the poor and lowly stepchild in business, will inevitably take the hit when something goes wrong. The "evil finger of blame" always points to IT, so CYA is the battle cry of the day. Any business and or IT project, enhancement, fix, or activity always has a plan and contingencies. To the naked eye, the IT resource seems to step up to the blank canvas and produce a masterpiece. Wrong. Multiple scenarios, work-arounds, and contingencies are documented, so at implementation the eleventh hour of hell does not rear its dastardly head.

I was at a major insurance company, and at that time I had spent several years in the business, and proceeded to hear, see, and document these observations for future use. I took note of what questions were posed to my peers and colleagues when they migrated from company to company for advancement. As with any topic of discussion, there are multiple viewpoints; this followed the prescribed path also.

All corporate establishments were looking at the immediate technical expertise needed at their company. However, business management was always looking for its counterparts: IT management. This is the norm. As I have said, many of us techies did not want to take the yellow brick road into "corporate babysitting"—sorry, I mean management. We wanted to keep our hands dirty working with the clay of our trade, the code. It is often said that if you enjoy what you do, then it really does not have all the negative connotations of a job. The everyday programmer or analyst just loves making the code do something productive for the business.

In the midst of all this activity and within the normality of the IT resources' daily grind, I saw then and growing exponentially the power of IT. Yes, power, real power. As for the computer—the actual physical piece of hardware that sits in a data center—its size and stature is becoming less cumbersome. Look at your own devices: desktops, to laptops, to tablets, to phones. Size is decreasing, and inversely the power is increasing exponentially. The power that I speak of is the metaphysical. The computer is in every aspect of our lives. We as humans have an umbilical cord attaching our bodies to a device. We cannot do anything if we do not have an electronic connection. The computer used to be an expensive, "nice to have" electronic thing; now it is a necessity that must be kept current.

As I have reiterated, there was and still is a bottomless pit of wants and needs by the business community to have IT perform its "magic" for the benefit of corporate management. IT's power has no obstacles or limitations; everything is doable with that black box. Technology does have some minor limitations; however, this is short term and is rectified very quickly. The power of that damn blasted black box, the computer, has invaded all aspects of the corporate world and our personal lives. Business was one front, and the personal lives of all of us was another; yes, we are entering a brave new world. Just look at today's world, and then look where we were a mere five years ago. The computer has enhanced or maybe hindered all us more and more. Yes, HAL is alive and kicking.

However, many American IT workers did not have the foresight or desire to fully harness and embrace this power. Complacency, trust, fear of rocking the boat, or just being fat, dumb, and happy with the current state of affairs kept many of us from being activists. Satisfaction does have its privileges; however, it does encourage complacency. Computers are in everything we do. I do not want to say that the public is a slave to the machine, but, yes, we sure are! The computer is not the main focus here, it's the software; the code that a programmer creates is vital, so very vital to all of us. I saw my position, at several major companies, come into almost panic mode when the systems crashed, mailings were missed, a report was wrong or not created, or data was mishandled. The business community was beside itself. No, I am not finger pointing with the blame factor, but the control, the total control of the business, was wanted by management; in fact they demanded it, now. This drove home the point, at least in my mind, that we, as IT resources, have a tremendous amount of power. Business hates to work or defend itself, especially when it's at fault. IT usually took the brunt of any blame; do not forget IT is the stepchild of business.

Stated a few paragraphs above, the power, the real power, of numbers coupled with an activity that is needed was shown in vivid Technicolor in the 1980s. While Ronnie Regan was the chief-cook-and-bottle-washer in charge of our fair land, the powerful air traffic controllers decided on a labor action. Yes, ye little one—a strike! That tool used by labor unions to disrupt the populace to get their demands met, their issues resolved, and their wants and needs resolved. Attention to an issue is brought into the limelight. They felt their management just wasn't listening, did not care, or was monetarily being a scrooge. I am not going into the validity of the controllers' concerns, management and their actions, or the labor action itself; what I am talking about is how this activity affected everybody. This relatively small group of individuals crippled a sig-nificant piece of our economy. Airplanes that transported parcels and people were significantly hampered, and since this is vital for our existence, we all were affected. IT has this same power, yet is a thousand times more powerful. Just look at your own life; this will tell you, in very emphatic terms, everything you need to know. We pay homage to HAL and R2-D2; the computer is in every facet of our lives. Yes, the computer is the god of the twenty-first century and beyond.

I am a business systems analyst. My focus is on systems, business and technical processes, and data within the company. An analyst looks at all the factors at hand, possible causes and effects on indices working on the factors, work-arounds, and the feasibility of the processes as they relate to the progression on our careers and what the company's possible paths could be. At one time my colleagues and I had a conversation, a poignant and volatile verbal exchange. I suggested the idea of organizing the IT resources into a union. My reasoning was that we, as IT, had a tremendous amount of power in our hands. Also, corporate management was getting antsy that they did not have the knowledge, power, resources, and management needed to control IT. My idea of unionizing was met with total disagreement not by management, but my peers, so much so that it was like I was committing an act of treason in the mere mentioning of *union*. The demographics of most IT professionals are college educated, professional, possibly a Republican, salaried, and think of themselves as non–blue collar resources. The origin of unions and organized labor in the United States, as it is documented in our history books, is nasty and horrible. Violence and more violence, labor against management, and "the sides have been drawn so let the war begin" were the past, not the future, of organized labor. The IT professional had taken these history classes and would rather not have repeated those atrocities, so avoidance was the chosen course. The IT professional was well compensated, in a respected profession, with his skills in demand and the world at his fingertips. Why organize when the ride is at optimum performance? That was what management showed us and what it kept showing the IT world until they were ready to strike. We were blinded by the light and an attitude of complacency. My peers were in agreement that organizing into a union was not needed or warranted. I abandoned my active approach; I however looked at and documented the factors at hand. My observations were as follows: computers were used in everything that we did, and more was being added daily; we had the power of numbers; corporate management wanted more for less; the abuse of power by management was beginning. I also recorded observations of other organized professions and my thoughts on the "what if" of future IT resources. I was not and am not advocating the overthrow of corporate leaders. I am a believer in "fair play". I saw and felt the rumblings of corporate management. I believe I did have the foresight to severely hinder and maybe stop this present-day outsourcing fiasco. I do not know and cannot prove my allegations that this action would have worked. As I said, hindsight is always twenty-twenty.

Americans get annoyed, to say the very least, at teachers, law enforcement officers, firemen, mailmen, sports professionals, and garbage men—all of whom are organized in unions—when they strike. Sometimes monetary issues or the unreasonable union demands are why the public is not happy with a labor action, but mostly it is the disruption of their own personal lives. Man does not like change; he prefers status quo, complacency if you wish. Man likes consistency. Man wants to see his life progress on calm seas, no more, no less. Change in the norm is difficult to accept, even for a short period of time. I had a sociology class in college. The professor was lecturing on the topic of social class as it related to menial labor. He mentioned a local transit strike causing havoc with the public. He mentioned the importance, the need for the respect of the public. Then I hit him with a curve ball. I said I agreed with all he said, but there was a labor action in NYC that he'd left out: the garbage men were on strike. We all look at this task as a menial, low-class job that drop-outs choose as a career path, a non-important activity taken for granted in our lives till they do not pick up the trash that we create. Then they are gods, and we will do anything to get them back on the street. My professor was speechless; however, he agreed with me and revised his notes.

We, the technological community, were lulled into accepting a false situation and thought it would never end and therefore were not prepared for the unexpected. We should have organized with the Teamsters or Longshoremen. Why them? Simple: both unions represent people who move parcels from point A to point B. IT moves data, the parcels of the technology era. The unions move their packages around the block or across the United States. IT moves and processes data internally within a company and externally to an outside company. Parcels of today are not limited to a physical product; information in the form of data is constantly in flux. IT is the present eighteen-wheeler trucking down the interstate.

A question to ponder is this: would organizing or unionization have prevented outsourcing? I would like to think that it would have; at the very least it would have curtailed or severally limit the mass influx of unqualified resources and kept our gainful employment here. Do not give me the bullshit line about the "global economy"—charity begins at home, and this is home, our home. Another bullshit excuse by corporations is the expansions of businesses into these third-world nations. To date I have not seen one insurance company going to India to insure the slums of Calcutta. It's all about the company. It's all about the money.

The power we had in IT was a good thing for the IT resource, probably—no, definitely. However, business did not like the forecast on manpower. Business, as I previously stated, has a love-hate attitude about what IT does for them, but losing control of the beast known as IT was not in the cards for common corporate management. After all, IT is Cinderella and the rest of business the stepsisters; those stepsisters were mean bitches and wanted everything.

17: Mothers, Don't Let Your Kids Grow Up to Become Cowboys

OMG—not another war story! I know I am sounding like your parents or long-lost relatives, but you have lasted with me this long; let's finish the ride. With age comes wisdom through experience.

I know in your journey through life you have heard the past acquaintances say, "Back when I was in school, I had to walk five miles each way". Good for you—it was an opportunity for character building. What I am saying is that my historical accounts are not BC, Revolutionary War era, or pre-historic; they are in the realm of today's IT environment. Which, in the scheme of things, means they're very current. I am not preaching. I bring realism, factualism, and reality to the forefront with the possibility of changing the story rather than reading about it in a historical account. Smoke 'em, if you got 'em.

Several years ago, I was on assignment at a major insurance company, working on several IT initiatives. One afternoon, a fairly intense conversation started up with several colleagues about our own current positions and other career choices. An interesting question was raised: would we recommend our current career choice to the next generation? Would we do it again? Also, what kind of direction could we give to the students entering higher education for their careers?

I can recall the response an associate made concerning her son, who was in the final stages of medical schooling and an intern at a hospital. To say the least it was shocking to me. At that time Obamacare, or the Affordable Care Act, was being argued, pushed thru, or sold to Congress and the American public. I was surprised at her take on it.

In thinking about the medical profession, I assumed it would be tense and trying but also rewarding, provided you had the money, time, stomach, and fortitude to get past the educational grind. I was wrong, so very wrong. She explained about the political bull her son had seen at some very large medical facilities, not the trials of just plain medicine. The hospital, the patient, and the insurance companies all had their views on medical care, each putting their own needs first. Oh yes, the "what about me?" principal. Economics is in the forefront of patient care according to all the secondary participants—not the primary participant, the patient. I guess I had been duped into thinking the opposite by those medical dramas on the boob tube; well, they were pure fiction. Got to love HIPAA. Then I considered my own physician. She was part of a group of doctors that I thought was great. Service was decent, there were no long hours of waiting, and personnel was very competent. However, there was that overlaying factor, not so apparent to the patients. It was medicine on a conveyor belt or assembly line. It was getting the patient in and out, a Jiffy Lube mentality. In that approach, time spent by the doctor on non-billable work is not important, but medicine is scary, confusing, unknown, and sometimes painful to the non-medical person, and time for compassion and understanding are needed by our doctors. She and several other medical professionals left. Now she has her own practice and appears to be very happy. My associate said that her son would not recommend the medical profession and that he would gladly get out except for the dollars wrapped up in school expenses.

The conversation then turned to me and IT. This group had some idea, if not a complete understanding of the details, about the outsourcing of IT positions. They also asked if this scenario was limited or widespread.

I expressed a very negative view of my once proud career choice. Education was an issue, but employment prospects were my main focus. The "IT world" gave me economic gains, but also it was fun to go into work. It was fun creating code and having that code do something that business needed and wanted. The cost of getting a computer science degree does not equate to economic payback following graduation. I am not saying that a college education is an entitlement for future employment. What I am saying is that knowledge is a big asset, and positions should go to the best candidate. I see nothing wrong with the foreign influence in major league sports. Why? They are the best, as opposed to outsourcing IT positions to less than third world bodies, which equates to corporate welfare under the auspices of the "global economy".

As for the pseudo-accolades presented to and about my foreign "counterparts" from the current business administration, well, I am in total disagreement without any reservations. The corporate line is not limited to a few select companies but is spouted by all. Even the consulting companies, once a vital cog in this machine, will talk to you, make the proverbial promises, and yet have a stable of foreigners for our positions. The American employment corporate culture, when it comes to IT, has completely focused on foreign labor and will hire only them. What was that, discrimination? At the motherland? That can't be!

I have been refused positions for which I know I have met or exceeded all the requirements. Why? Because I like baseball, hot dogs, apple pie, and Chevrolet; yes, because I am an American. So would I recommend IT? Do you really need to ask?

18: It Is Halftime, We're Down by Two Touchdowns. Coach, What Are We Going to Do?

It halftime, the game is on the verge of being a blowout, but we get the ball first in the next half. What is the game plan, coach? The ever-positive coach states, "This is how I see this fiasco playing out," and then spells out his vision as if he had a crystal ball. Okay, it might just be positive thinking on the coach's part, or he has seen something, or "it's not over till the fat lady sings." Whatever, it ain't over till it's over, and this outsourcing war can and must be won. I really want to say this and believe this—I must! The flip side is far worse to imagine or think about.

I am an avid believer in fighting the battles you can win and conceding the others; to do otherwise is only wasted, futile efforts. Yes, this may seem a David-and-Goliath situation here; however, this tide of inferior technical staff must be stopped. Upper education is a necessity in life, but a computer science degree—a once highly coveted degree—is now worth less than dog shit. Is this good for America? A resounding, *hell no*! Rather than getting oneself into major debt with no foreseeable way of recouping the monetary sacrifice, become a plumber. Have you seen what they charge per hour? Besides, going to the bathroom is totally free of all economic restraints.

In addition to no viable means of a career prospect, I feel the following is even much more devastating to us as a country. We are living a technological world. Everything we do revolves around some sort of technology. We were the leader. We were the best. We are regressing fast to a bottomless pit of has-beens. Our technology should be propagated, nurtured, and advanced or else we will become a nation of twitters. The only way is education and the use of this education to hone our technological expertise.

The average American will change careers several times by the time he gets to retirement age, so be flexible. The past corporate tenure where you spent twenty-five, thirty, thirty-five, or more years for a company is now the exception. This is not your parents' career path, though maybe it should be. Learn this early and learn it fast: life is not fair, never was, and never will be.

Americans are resilient. Americans are a group of souls that want the first, the best, and want the newest of everything. Adversity is nothing new to the American public; we do what we have to do to survive. Yes, we all bitch and moan, but when push comes to shove, I will take us anytime. If not immediately, we do it over time. Maybe we should take a play out of the corporate playbook. We live, in their vernacular, in a "global economy", so we should embrace the outsourcing line, perhaps through the possible curriculum listed below. A local university or on-line program will grant you a B.S. in Monkeyology leading to a masters or doctorate. Hell, as Gloria Gaynor sang so successfully, "I Will Survive".

Since the gods of corporate blue with pinstripes have deemed the third-world nation superior when it comes to the computer, we as Americans must make the proverbial lemonade from lemons. This is the curriculum.

First let me define Monkeyology. It is the study of the elusive code monkey, and through our own capitalism principals we can overcome. The not so mythical being known as the code monkey was created by corporate America to assume the positions of the

American IT resource. This curriculum may be tongue in cheek, or it may be real. You decide its direction.

The following is a curriculum of study leading to a degree in Monkeyology. Yes, a MCMBA, Masters in Code Monkey Business Administration. Corporate America has established the ground rules, so let's play ball. Batter up!

- CM100: Introduction to Monkeyology
A cursory examination into what Monkeyology is. Tutorial view of how the code monkey was introduced into the American business and why. Where the species can be found. What the species looks like. Variations of the code monkey in behavior and disposition.

- CM150: History of Monkeyology
The code monkey's origin; where did he come from? The code monkey's beginning—was it ape or test tube to man-like form? In-depth discussions into the theories of evolution of the code monkey and what brought this species into life. How and why did he land his spaceship or pod here? This will be an in-depth and critical study of the code monkey from inception to present day.

- CM175: Brave New World of the Code Monkey and Humanoids
Associate or enemy, an intoxicating view of where we are today. Where we are headed? The code monkey is here; how is he adapting to his new environment physically? What are the emotional traits of the monkey? What are the economics that surround the monkey, here and abroad? Can man coexist with this species; if so how? Does the phenomenon exist purely in America?

- CM200: The Psychology of the Code Monkey: Sociopath or Blessing
What makes him tick? What are his likes? Dislikes? Cohabitation with man—is it possible?

- CM210: Developmental Psychology of the Code Monkey
The code monkey's mental and psychological development. What internal and external forces work on this organism? What the code monkey extrudes into their environment.

- CM250: Detrimental Aspects of the Code Monkey to the Monkey
Is the monkey beneficial to American society? Is he beneficial to his native habitat? Will this brave new world collapse on us, or on them? Two opposing life forces, what are the negative forces on man? On monkey? Conversely, what are the positive forces?

- CM300: Behavior Modification of the Code Monkey: Potty Training 101
Proven techniques in the training of these resources as it relates to the American way.

- CM325: Introduction of Technology to the Code Monkey
The code monkey is a biological phenomenon; technology is not inherent to the species. The positive and negative effects of introducing the code monkey to and training him to use technology. How to replicate 'a golden child of IT' in terms useful to the IT world.

- CM350: Physical and Psychological Attributes of the Code Monkey
Expound on the differences within the species. The American way of life as it relates to the code monkey, a cause and effect of the American versus the homeland ways, and possible treatment for the code monkey.

- CM361: Common Ailments and Afflictions of the Code Monkey
Everyday, common, and repeatable maladies and suggested treatments.

- CM401: Metamorphosis of the American IT Worker Caused by the Code Monkey

How did the American IT worker change with the introduction of the code monkey? Discussion of the adverse effects and decreased productivity of the American IT worker.

- CM402: Code Monkey Management

Techniques to obtain maximum utilization of the code monkey resource. Modern-day slavery, as practiced by corporate America.

- CM403: Plantation

Selected family members, loyal to the confederate flag and Robert E. Lee, in a symposium of life in the pre–Civil War South. How do the two situations parallel and differ? Review of what is happening and prognosis of what will happen.

- CM450: Ethics: Moral, Racist, or Darwinism? The Evolution of I Bake Muffins

Is the code monkey superior? HAL, R2-D2, and C3-PO are overtaking man.

- CM475: Species variations

Sociological, physiological, ethnic, and psychological variations. Differences and similarities. Do they work? Are they intrinsic enemies?

- CM500: Code Monkey Husbandry

Getting your first few couples is easy but costly. Knowing how and what to breed is advantageous to your autonomy. The American pimp and his harem as it would be. What are the pitfalls and rewards of breeding the species for the owner?

- CM550: Code Monkey Breeding

This is the practical that goes along with course CM500. This is a year-long class from insemination to birth.

- CM600: Code Monkey's Agenda

Is there a bigger, ultimate game plan? If so, what is the plan, when or what time line and where is ground zero or has it yet to be?

- CM800: Code Monkeys for Fun and Profit

The use and management of the code monkey was once a cottage industry or hobby venture but now full-fledged companies utilize the code monkey as a product. Step by step instructions on how to accomplish this. This class will cover common business issues and pitfalls, including tax ramifications and federal and local laws and regulations. The new, emerging market as touted by the business pros—is this for real or just a fad?

- CM801: Marketing and Business Strategies

Code monkeys are utilized in the American business. How do they fare in the foreign markets?

- CM825: The Art of the Negotiation

Foreign or domestic supplies. Difference and similarities. Unholy alliances and business maneuvers must be learned and executed to grow your stable of golden monkeys.

- CM826: Playing the American Game

The game of business. What is it? How is it played? Code monkey; player, owner, asset, liability, or agenda? How does he fit in? Business language, processes, and mores are at the forefront in United States businesses. Laws and regulations must be learned and played to perfection. The basic objective of business is the acquisition money, and that governs how resources are obtained and used. Many Americans are novices on Wall Street; the gamesmanship of how and when to apply pressure and clout to get the upper hand is examined.

- CM850: I Was a Poor Third-World Inhabitant

An expose of an actual living and working code monkey now a "golden child" of IT working for the man.

- CM875: The Code Monkey: Is It Worth the Price?

American business is the prime residence and recipient of the code monkey; is his cost justified? ROI analysis of this experiment is used to discuss the question, are the costs just too high, or do we sacrifice quality for profits?

- CM900: Importing and Exporting the Commodity
American business has made the code monkey's services into a commodity. Marketing? Legality? Laws?

- CM950: IT training for the Code Monkey.
Introduction into IT. What is IT? Logic, the basis of IT.

- CM960: IT training for the Code Monkey. Intermediate.
COBOL, JCL, specifications, testing procedures, databases. Hands on with present business issues.

- CM970: IT training for the Code Monkey. Advanced.
Working with your business counterparts. Find out what the customer really wants. System creation. Team working.

19: The Rise and Fall of the Roman Empire

Great civilizations and governments all have been toppled by poor management, politics, religion, policy, or war. This same affliction is happening within businesses of today. American corporations have become as complacent as American IT professionals were before outsourcing. Apparently corporate management is dumber than I thought. The affliction is not readily apparent to the business gods or thought as even being an issue. As a matter of fact, businesses seem to think that they have everything under control and well in hand. Oh, wee little one, what you do not see can and will kill you! Not figuratively but metaphorically, but the dire end is as disastrous as war, an all-out war, comparable to any of the World Wars. Perhaps this war does not result in death or destruction in the physical sense, but an all-out financial war is being waged.

Businesses have assumed the position and are on their way to total self-destruction, and it is all being done by themselves and to themselves. Why? The answer is simple: pure and unadulterated greed. Yes, sir, Mr. Gekko, "that greed, for lack of a better word, is good", but at what cost? Businesses and their poor decisions on IT, are in the midst of this self-degradation. I feel present corporate management "can't see the forest for the trees". Yes, on the surface businesses appear to have all their ducks neatly in rows, but do they? This is war, and there most definitely will be casualties. The only questions are who and how many, but I have no doubt the carnage will be astronomical.

I have already nuked the notion of a "global economy"; let's get on with it. I do not feel any sympathy for the foreign invaders—would they if the sides were reversed? Today's business climate must be addressed at full gallop and head on; there is no time for a learning curve. We are Americans working in America; speak and understand the language, or get the hell out and go back into the hole you came from. Yes, they are products of third, fourth, and nth worlds—not my problem. The business world is not a charity operation; it is, pure and simple, capitalism. This is the major league—survive or die.

Nothing in IT is ever permanent; growth within the technology sector is happening at warp speed. Two factors, no matter whether the IT resources are foreign or domestic, are the tangible concerns: time and money. Corporations will spend the money, but they want guarantees. Yep, guarantees. They know what systems can do for them presently. Can something new get the same results without placing the business in jeopardy? In terms of cost, if significant money is spent, will it be recouped, and will the business make more money? All these major issues, all these questions, cannot be answered to the satisfaction of corporate management. I have another question. Are the foreign IT gurus up to the task? Do they have the abilities, not just on paper, but do they actually have the education and talent to do it? I think not. No, I know emphatically and unequivocally that they are totally substandard. If what corporate management says it's true, that foreign IT resources are at least equal or better than the home team; then why haven't they tackled major IT tasks or wants? I think corporate management has this one right by holding back. I think a major revisions in their thinking and propaganda are at hand. Give one to corporate blue.

These systems or processes will be replaced when push comes to shove; like Y2K, that dirty, old COBOL is there and working well. The technical resources presently at hand are not talented, and the business community has always and will continue to be skeptical of change. The old will continue to rule till the old is in a walker and probably will still be when I am pushing up daisies.

Business has started on the journey of self-destruction by importing a major number of foreign and unqualified technical IT resources and fooling—in truth, lying to—themselves, saying that they are a superior resource. Yes, my friend Billy sums it up: "the lady doth protest too much". In actuality I think they, corporate executives, are still trying to convince themselves. Good luck. The quality of the foreign resource can be summed up by a well-known saying: you get what you pay for. Business has always been focused on the "dead presidents", and that is the whole story, plain and simple. Now, folks, you are all Harvard grads with an MBA.

Cost is the primary focus of business. The lack of technical expertise and intangibles like communication, attitude, and work ethic are all major deficits of the cheap foreign IT resource product from overseas. The foreign counterparts are "all about me" in all that they do. They value self-growth and advancement over what the business needs and wants. The foreign IT resource has not sold, nor will they sell, their souls to the business as the American has. They just want to rape the businesses of experience and money. The comparison between foreign and domestic resources overwhelming favors the domestic.

American businesses and how they work are not unique, though they are in some respects. The way things are said, the company's agenda or direction, the criticality of products, corporate knowledge, and keeping it close to the vest are ideals of the American way of doing business. The foreign resource has no idea about, care for, nor loyalties to corporate America. Look at identity theft. This did not appear till we opened our systems to any and everybody. The Internet is great, but it spawned a tremendous amount of bad. You want the Internet? Well, it's a package deal. My tenure in systems has allowed me to see and use sensitive data; I did not steal it and dispense it to the highest bidder. We all believed in what we did. We all had integrity. We all respected the data.

Technology growth will continue as long as there are systems, basically for eternity. Yep, the monkey is out of the box, and the box has been "nuked". Americans strive for superiority in what they do, and they do it very well. These third-world resources can barely spell their names, much less understand business concepts and create complex code to have the blessed computer do what is needed. Yes, they are dummies, and I make no apologies for this statement. Do not give me the liberal point of view that we must coddle the foreign; sorry, Charlie, business takes no prisoners. They are not the "golden children" of IT, as business management would have us believe. We as a nation are losing our superiority in technology and giving it away based on the false premise of being part of a global economy; hell no, we have instituted global welfare.

What I have noticed, and what appears not to be apparent to corporate leaders, is the transfer of power. Corporate management, who are bringing in more and more foreign resources, are being looked at, studied, and then made the target of planned takeover by the same people they brought in. Yep, the so-called solution is the source of a bigger issue, and it is rearing its ugly head. Do not lose sight of the "what about me?" factor. The foreign resources' agenda is to help the motherland, a motherland that is overpopulated, poor, and with an economy that is in the shitter. So why not attack the hand that feed you? You see where their loyalties are. Global economy? Hell no; it's about them and them only. In retrospect, if I or we were in a depressed part of our world where work, growth, or just existence was at risk daily, I too would sell my soul to the devil for a glass of water. My issue is not with them but with our corporate management, who blindly exploit for gains.

Business is on a suicidal path similar to a junkie hooked on his vice of choice. He has done it before, and he assumes he can do it again and again to achieve the same euphoria. Well, sometimes—and usually always—the clock runs out. Business has been propagating the so-called global economy, bullshit with a capital *B*.

American companies with international relationships advertise at American sporting events, promoting the perception that a global alliance of brotherhood and solidarity in a cohesive working structure is good for all. Bullshit! This is America. I really do not want to go hand in hand and sing "Kumbaya" while he has my job in my homeland. Go back to your hole in the ground. These companies both assume an American heritage and use substandard resources. Propagation and perception are their key attributes.

The biggest reason that this business behavior could, should, and can be reversed is that this social, business, and economic experiment is an epic failure with devastating results. Americans, for the most part, do not care about nations thousands of miles away; they care about their homeland and what is outside the back doors. A sign of good political leader is that his constituents are happy. Happiness equates to jobs. Americans want one thing, and that thing is to work so that they can put food on the table, buy a house, buy that new thing, save some money, and just be American. Our politicians will change their views; it might take time, but they care about their cushy jobs on Capitol Hill. Loud and consistent voices will buck this trend; and oh yes, it is always about the money.

20: I Shot the Sheriff. But I Didn't Shoot No Deputy

Truly, if you are a diehard capitalist, purely interested in your monetary well-being, you surely have already banished me to hell. My sentiments are the same; however, if you are open-minded and willing to read, think, and agree with or challenge my views, I say thanks.

I do intensively detest the foreign IT resource. Their lack of competencies, their language failure, their customs, their behavior, their "what about me?" attitude, basically everything about them is out of tune with America. Some would say I am a racist. Well, maybe I am, but in reality I am an American, a capitalist, a strong proponent of labor, and a student of fair play.

And really, folks, are not we all a little racist? How many times have we bitched and moaned when we called for some technical support for our own home computers, phones, or any device using a computer chip and got one of those "golden children" trying to help? Frustrating at all levels, starting with communications. At times, probably all if not most times, are like oil and water; they just do not mix.

These foreign IT resources are what we see, talk to, or interact with are the tangible signs in our daily lives. It's like rubbing salt in an open wound. The real enemy or foes are the CEOs, CIOs, presidents, and boards of directors at these major companies who brought in the foreign IT resources.

The following is stated with my capitalist hat on, so hold on to your collective asses. Any company has the right, indeed, the directive to be profitable, to be number one. Therefore, outsourcing, on the surface, looks to be a good thing for business, but is it? Business wants the formula that represents the business to be totally unbalanced. As Burger King said many years ago, "have it your way". They were talking about the hamburger, but the sentiments are the same. It's like when one team has all the best players and the others have the rejects. Yes, they will win, but it really isn't fun to watch. Business wants to produce a product at the cheapest means available. In conjunction with manufacturing these products, business wants the home populace to buy their products. This is the same home populace that had their employment and livelihood stolen under the auspices of capitalism. Yes, businesses want to have their cake and eat it too.

The head flunkies leading us, no matter whether they are in a red or blue state, wave the banner for outsourcing. They always say that the global economy is good for America and technical advancement. Hey, Obama. Hey, Georgie. Hey, Billie. Get out of your cushy chairs in the library or stop fucking some broad and see the masses, talk with the masses, and do what we asked for without worrying about political correctness. Say what the truth is; don't give use a selected, political-ad sound bite. Hey, was it not we, the same masses, that put you in the hallowed halls of Washington? This is the Donald's game plan. He does not play by the petty rules of politics. No secret agenda. No sound bite. I respect him for telling it like it is. Yes, he is wealthy. Yes, he is arrogant to the nth degree. Yes, he is not politically correct. Yes, he does have faults. He's probably a liar—aren't they all? Is he wrong in what he says? In his eyes, no. He is no politician. I believe he truly wants America off life support.

I am a big fan of the NFL, the Giants particularly. Every game day I am religiously at my television or at the game. My wife doesn't understand my "fan mania" and loyalty obsession, especially during the lean times—of which there have been a few. I loyally partake in cheering on the team, no matter what. The team is not just players who are the field; it's the coaches, the manager, the GM, and the owners. It is a cohesive unit, all playing their respective parts to produce a winning team. If any area is faulty, it will tend to result in a bad product. A case in point is the Dallas Cowboys. Before you readers go ballistic on me, let me explain. I am a Giant fan, so it's obvious that I hate the Cowboys—, it's in my blood, a natural thing. But let us look at the Cowboys and their problems. The players are a good mix of stars and rookies. They are your typical team facing typical problems with personalities, the law, and playing abilities; all teams have these issues. Head coaches are on a revolving door or conveyor belt with America's Team. Proven big-name coaches avoid this team. Why? Prospective coaches are available, money is not an issue, Dallas is not a bad place to play, they have big stadium, and the cheerleaders are the gold standard. So, then, why the turnover? It is my contention that they are a dysfunctional team. The dysfunction is a product of their owner; Jerry Jones is the problem. In Jerry's defense, he is extremely rich, I am not, and therefore he can do what he wants to whomever he wants whenever he wants. Basically, he can tell me to stick it up my ass, and he probably will. I digress. Owners, good owners, spend money on quality personnel. Each person knows his or her duties and responsibilities and so just do it. Jerry wants to be a player's friend. He is the owner and not a friend. He sticks his nose in areas that he should not, second-guessing coaching decisions, player personnel issues, game issues, and the press. Yes, Jerry wants to be one of the boys. All this puts unneeded pressure on his staff; everything is scrutinized, seconded-guessed, and questioned. This is tolerated when the team is winning, but its hell when the team is losing. My recommendation for the ultimate success of the Cowboys is that Jerry sell his team. As I said, fight the battles you can win. I have a better chance winning the lottery than that happing. So I do take solace in this dysfunctional team: after all, they play the Giants two times per season, and this non-chemistry helps my team. I will take any advantage at any time. These sentiments are paralleled by business, completely! Corporate executives have tunnel vision and really do not care about anything other than their little baby, the business. As I said, the sole purpose of a business is to make more and more money, no matter the means.

21: Kryptonite

Superman has kryptonite as his nemesis; business has something that is good and bad at the same time, and that is money. Business is a bit like a sex addict or food addict. Man needs sex and food to survive, but too much of an obsession with either is detrimental to man's life. Yes, any business has one main objective: make money. Make money to support the workforce, allow product expansion and development, make the market watchers happy and eager to invest, and—we dare not forget—make the execs a boatload of dead presidents. Yes, more money. Businesses like money, but in terms of psychology, it can and usually becomes an OCD, an obsessive-compulsive disorder. Once the business gets a taste of the blood, the money that is, it wants more and more. An analogy to this is a bear. If a bear gets a taste of human blood, then he gets obsessed with it and wants more and more; the bear then has to be put down to protect the public.

Money is not the root of all evil; casinos are not bad because some people have a trouble with controlling their own issues. Liquor stores should not revert back to the days of prohibition because we have alcoholics; all of us are not in that state. We, Americans, have issues with pharmaceuticals, both recreational and medical. Okay, then, do we close all the pharmaceutical companies for a few junkies? No, that is not going to happen. Business needs money to stay alive, more is good, and obsession with money or anything is bad.

We, as a society, have a problem with outsourcing, a large one that looks daunting, probably big enough that facing off against it is fighting a battle we can't win and so therefore a battle we should concede. However, that philosophy on concession is not an option here; we have to win this battle. The damage being done by corporate greed has far more implications than putting American out of work and the missing of the projected earnings for the stock market. The following are factors to ponder:

- The US economy: Businesses like to think in terms of autonomy—they are the only one, and nothing else matters. Unfortunately they, business, can't act like two-year-olds; they have to share their toys. If all businesses give employment positions to the outside world, then they have all the money and we do not. The economy fails.

- Outsourcing: On the surface it looks like a no-brainer for corporations, and in some cases it is. Cafeteria, grounds keeping, and house cleaning look fine for this. IT services are something else. IT, even though corporate management hates to admit it, works very close with its counterparts, the business side of the house. Intimate information is shared and worked with on a daily basis. The "IT staff" becomes more intimately connected with business operations as time goes by, as the two worlds merge as one.

- Technology: We were the leader; however, we are losing the ground between number one and two. We were and should be the gold standard for this. Yes, we should be the dominant force. Technology, not legions of video game players, will lead us into the future.

- Education: The woes of upper education include professors in their ivory towers and cushy jobs and tuition that is, well, out of this world. Professors need to understand practicality, the real world, not just theory. Without an educated society our nation will regress to third-world status.

In some respects we have that now. We preach that we are number one, but we aren't.

- Outsourcing others services: We outsource IT now; how about engineering, medicine, science, or the law. We are becoming a nation of receivers and not doers. We are getting complacent and not authoritative.

- Foreign replacement of a college-educated populace: We will, in the not so distant future, pledge allegiance to India, China, or any other third-world nation. Trust me; discussions as to the worth of a college degree are going on now. Why spend $200,000 or more to get a mortgage payment for student loans but no viable employment position that you trained for? If we aren't already, we are becoming a second-class nation.

- Perks and benefits: Our US corporations always want tax breaks, benefits, anything and everything for their businesses benefit. They want to have their cake and eat it too. Let's change the rule and say that business must pay to play. Give these perks to loyal US companies and take them away or charge for eliminating US jobs.

- Claims that the foreign IT worker is better than local talent: That is a lie, promoted by business, on par with the check is the mail. Yes, we have European hockey players, and baseball has Cubans, Dominicans, and the Japanese, but they are superbly talented. Basketball has the occasional foreign influence, yet when their talents are compared to those of the United States, American talent is the gold standard.

- So-called local IT talent shortage: Business says that we do not have enough local IT talent to help our industries. When the lying starts, it creates an avalanche of bull. American IT workers have been told by their management to train their foreign replacements before they get laid off. Yes, the man has spoken—may I have another? I was at a local insurance company for a pre-contract interview. The project manager sorely needed my services. I was skeptical about his abundance of enthusiasm and questioning, so I became the aggressor. I asked for details about my pending position, questions that I knew he did not want to answer. He stated that the Americans had been phased out and they now had to do the work. Apparently they could not. I like it when I am right. And yes, I refused the assignment.

- Outsourcing: This is nothing new. Businesses in the United States always positioned and repositioned themselves in a better way, but it was different; they stayed within our borders. Labor and the economy always benefited; this is no longer true with this new approach.

- Global economy: Bullshit! We have to take care of number one—that is, us. Companies giving work to other nations does not help us. Many of us use airlines for travel. The safety briefing, which we all get and usually sleep through before we begin our journey, talks about an oxygen mask dropping when the cabin air pressure gets too low. It is always said to take care of yourself before you help another. That may not be too Christian, but it is oh so true. Global economy equates to global welfare.

- Union breaking: The labor unions do have some value. I like to say that everybody or everything has some redeeming qualities. So do not be so quick to throw out the baby with the bath water.

- The unfairness of life: I agree, but let's kick the asses of the others not our own.

- Progression: Continuation of this behavior, outsourcing technical jobs to foreign resources, is a yellow brick road to hell, or perhaps I should say the bread lines of depression.

- Equality: As with a Utopian society, this concept is neither universally accepted nor wanted, and nor does it even exist. People have always accepted the premise of one-upmanship, being better than your fellow man. This is reality; again, it may be non-Christian, but it so very, very true.

The issues and problems are well documented. I enjoy hearing competent and educated people talk; emotion is left out, and the facts are enunciated. Mike Francesca is a sports journalist and has a never-ending knowledge of sports and the business of sports. I heard a statement he made regarding major league contracts and player movement between teams; he said, "It's always about the money", and he is so right. As the song goes, "money makes the world go round". Almost every legal proceeding comes down to some sort of cash judgment, be it divorce, death, fraud, or littering; the answer is simple and right in front of our noses. Monetary penalties should be awarded to the corporations who detract from our economy.

All corporations in the United States are guilty of outsourcing. I do not care about their excuses or reasoning; the bottom line is the same: US labor gets screwed, and we the public get screwed also. Take auto insurance. We all need it and buy it; in some cases it is even mandatory that we have it. And yet all these companies have outsourced their services. Yes, folks, they have their cake and can eat it too. Corporations know the game and have stacked the deck in their favor. Boycotting the products of one business or even a few of them will not work, since the entire business community is problem.

Businesses' allies—the government and politicians—are as guilty of obsession with money as are businesses. Congress, its members masked as statesmen, is a masquerade ball. They are not doing their civic duty for a better nation; they are out for themselves, and business knows this. Money is funneled through corporations and lobbies to our "government Cosa Nostra" for favorable business considerations. Let's take the recent discussion on gun control. The proposed legislation focused on the mental health of individual purchasing a gun. This legislation was not the sole task that would end gun violence, it was a start. According to the president and press an overwhelming majority of US citizens want this, so it should be a no-brainer for Congress to do something. But Congress, hiding behind a Second Amendment right issue, has refused to do anything. The real reason is the NRA with deep pockets; money talks and nobody walks.

This task of changing our greedy corporate enemies can be accomplished. What I have found to work in cases where the odds seem overwhelmingly against me is the power of the press. The pen is more powerful than the sword, and its use will not make you Bubba's girlfriend in your local penal system. It may appear on the surface that business has no formidable foes. Not so quick there, Speedy. Businesses' most dreaded enemy is negative press. When the papers, Internet, television, or radio get a story, they beat it like a dead horse. Then businesses' fair-weather friends come out of the woodwork, and Congress has the dreaded and televised show called the "hearing". This is better than *Judge Judy*, for it's real. This is reality television at its best. The best thing about this is that it is free, no-cost advertising; the article mentions names of companies or individuals, how the issue affects the average Joe or Jane, any peripheral effects, the possible outcome and long-term effects, and what is going to be done to rectify the situation. The court of public opinion might be misguided, but it is leaps and bounds above *Law and Order*; there are no rules, no requirements about proof. Look at the recent activity around Bill Cosby. Yes, America's dad. His alleged sexual exploits and cover-ups are fodder for everybody. The manmade loophole of the statute of limitations might technically save his ass. Public opinion, however, has made his legacy, his epitaph. Need we say more? In the court of public opinion, maybe we have our replacement for the stoic judges on the Supreme Court.

I like to believe we have a voice, a very loud voice, to turn treasonous policies around for the good of all of us.

22: Let's Go to the Video Tape

The outsourcing epidemic is the issue at hand and is the epicenter of our problem and not the solution as corporate leaders and our governmental flunkies want us to believe. Even though you and I have not created this issue directly, we must address it. Yes, our problem! Business must be tempered with some kind of controls, be it law, taxes, or government. If businesses are left to their own devices, well, we have anarchy. No person is immune from this epidemic.

Outsourcing proponents have used positive adjectives to market this behavior. The false and quick gains realized in the stock market will reverse. When this tide change happens, the sub-prime mortgage fiasco will be a mere blip on the radar.

I stated that business is war, yes war. In war there is casualties. Wars do have a pseudo economy. While the war goes through time, people do make financial gains from selling products to fight the war to the actual outcome of the war. Yes war is profitable, but short lived. Once peace is achieved, the economy reverts back to prewar status. No more bullets, bombs, or missiles are needed. As I said a temporary uptick in the market. Business equates to war this way. The business wants to sell all the widgets it can make at the lowest possible cost. Great, that is the universal business equation. But how a business lowers it costs is the important factor here. Yes outsourcing on the surface look great. I will give in on this fallacy for the moment, and that is the foreign IT resources quality of their work is the same as the American. So we have replaced our workers with the opposition. Now Mr. Businessman you want me, an unemployed worker, from your company, to buy your product. I think not. No money, I will do without. What does business gain? A warehouse full of widgets collecting dust.

One might say, well, this is an IT issue, and I am not in IT, so I am immune. Right you are, grasshopper. Any business has two key attributes. First, a business is dynamic, constantly changing and adapting like clay in the sculptor's hand. Second, a business is a creature of habit. Business does not like to go where it has not been. The unknown is left to Star Trek. Businesses have outsourced the food workers, building maintenance, and other services within their company. The limit is the sky. It worked in those areas, and then IT became the next objective. Question: what is next? It will happen, the only question is when. Business has an insatiable appetite for cash and will never be satisfied, and yes, there is no vaccine.

Another paradox of outsourcing involves the stock market. Yes, the stock market, the gold standard for capitalism, the benchmark by which all corporations are measured. It was previously mentioned that you and I are not directly responsible for the expansion of outsourcing. This is true. Indirectly, though, it is another story. Those of us who deal with the stock market for financial gains, and that is all of us in some form, want our investments to grow and create wealth; however, we mostly do not delve into the particulars of an investment. Maybe we should. Okay, you say I am not in the market; yes, but you are a consumer, and that is all of us. So yes, we do have a vested interest in the issue. As with any war—and this is war—a false economy blossoms in support of the military efforts. However, once the military efforts subside, then the economy reverts back. The same parallels can be drawn with outsourcing. Sure the companies' financials look great at first, but the true consumer, who has lost his employment position, will cut back his spending, thus the company gains are not realized for the long term.

Another indirect connection by the populace to outsourcing is through mutual funds. Yes, by investing in 401(k) s and our own financial game plans, we as unknowing participants are fueling and benefiting from this epidemic. All mutual funds do have a game plan; the prospectuses try to explain this plan in such boring terms that paint drying is more fascinating to watch. For example we have growth funds, income funds, energy funds, precious metal funds, and so forth. What has been touted for years, with certain aspects hidden so eloquently; were the emerging market funds. We all took part in the investing and capital gains of these funds, but what are they? Very simple: it's a PC name for third- and lesser-world nations. Emerging markets are a group of nations coming of age in the twenty-first century, poor, undeveloped areas of our planet that were confirmed or bar/bat mitzvahed into the brave new world. Business saw its next vital source of assets: dumb schmucks, people that could be utilized for business uses all under the idea of economic growth. Yes, modern-day slavery is alive and well.

Yes, these funds invested in the internal growth of these countries. Almost a parallel of the subprime mortgage condition, the lacking of prudence and control, money was dumped into undeveloped nations so that we could harvest a product. The product was the country's people. To use a term I despise the "global economy", this has been given the blessing of Wall Street, Corporate America, Madison Avenue, and all related business sectors, free and untethered access of a major commodity of all third-world nations, its people. Yes, these people were uneducated about the modern times and lived in deplorable conditions, and yes, they were primed for the picking—or better stated, exploitation—and they did not see it coming. I like to say it was "killing them with kindnesses". Many IT firms sent teaching armies to these candidates; they were like deer looking at headlights coming at them, mesmerized and dead in their tracks.

Last but far from least is that technology has a significant connection. In today's world, this tool, resource, or phenomenon of technology is used by all. You cannot do anything without it; we are all tethered at the hip literally or virtually. You may not be a techie of any sorts, but you do have a connection to the issue.

I focus on third-world labor resources, but this is not the real problem; it is only what we as the gilded public sees. The real issue is the lack of control on business. Before the hand of social-ism come crashing down on my head, as I have said previously and most fervently, I do believe in capitalism. Yet sometimes capitalism must be controlled, tempered for its own good. We have all heard that "too much of a good thing is bad"; well, we have it here and now.

I do believe that our economy was hit twice because of the lack of controls on Wall Street caused major financial meltdowns. First, the stock market crash of 1929, the starting point of the Great Depression, was devastating to all, not just to people who played the markets. Participants were allowed to buy stocks on margin, or in laymen's term credit. Ah yes, you play with the devil, you die with the devil. Buying stocks on margin is not like going to your local department store, buying whatever, and slapping it on your AmEx card. Several facts are relevant here: most people do not understand the stock market, there are too many people in the market who are not ready for it, most people want to do good for themselves, the stock market is a form of legalized gambling, and finally the rules of the stock market game make organized crime look like a game of checkers. The stock market has rules the ordi-nary man did not know, listen to, or abide by. The result was the crash where all the king's men could not put it back together. Yes, the Humpty Dumpty effect.

Then we have the more recent experiences with sub-prime mort-gages. I am of the firm belief that anyone who wants to buy a house should have this dream, as long as he qualifies for the funds to pay for it. The banks had this procedure in order, but greed and stupidity took over. Financial institutions and hedge fund manag-ers got greedy and were free to act on their greed because of lax government controls. And the public, who for the most part are stupid and gullible, were sucked right in and lost. The results were devastating.

If the bankers adhered to what rules they had in place or looked at the possible effects of negative market actions, these devastating events could have been, should have been avoided. Outsourcing is on the same destructive path.

The problem is the same as the solution. A person who has an eating disorder has a problem that will lead to bigger health issues, but a person needs to eat, or else he dies. This is the same scenario with many addictions, including capitalism.

23: A Spoonful of Sugar

There are two sides to addressing an issue, any issue. First, you state and describe the problem or issue; second, you give a possible solution or solutions. Otherwise, like most, it's just complain, complain, and complain. A therapist was a guest lecturer in a psychology course I took many, many, many moons ago; he said some people just like to bitch and hear themselves complain. I am not one of them. I have stated the problem, and I most definitely have a solution.

Some businesses, like the auto insurance business, appear to have a monopoly in this outsourcing crap. I like to call it "have the cake and eat it phenomenon". The auto insurance industry has this scenario: insurance is a mandatory requirement for operating a motor vehicle, so the insurance companies know we need it and we must have it to be compliant with the states' laws. Thus the big red umbrella, Lawrence the stag, good hands people, Flo, or the General, to state a few, can and do what they want business-wise and get away with it. Lest we forget, we all know the intimate relationship that Americans have with their cars. We all need that piece of paper, an insurance policy, to operate a motor vehicle legally. Let us not lose site of the big picture; this is happening in all businesses, not just auto insurance, under the auspices of capitalism.

We are at a place in our civilization where everybody gets there, no matter what. This is "the law of the circle of life". What is that?

Well, wee grasshopper; it's not the *Lion King*. This law mimics what happens in nature: small animals are dinner for larger ones. It may sound cruel, but it is oh so very true. In corporate America, there is carnage, a kind of death. A company wants to have a monopoly in a product, but capitalism and competition come into play. Anyway, sell more while cutting costs is the mantra. This is a viable model; however, it is one of diminishing returns. Either business schools do not teach this vital concept, or students do not grasp it. While all I said is true—selling more and decreasing the cost of the product are vital for all businesses to survive—the how portion, how to achieve the cost reduction of said product, is a very slippery slope. As was stated in the "Ten Commandments of Corporate Blue", all people are expendable. However, if you cut vital manpower, whatever that is for said product, and you cut vital input of dollars, it will diminish your bottom line rather than increase it. The products produced in the United States are used in first-world countries, not in lesser worlds. Yes, this sounds like ethnic oppression, but it's true. As an insurance company, would you sell auto insurance in New Delhi? Have you seen their drivers, their road system, or the laws governing use of autos, if any? They appear to be nonexistent, at least to American standards. This is a major lose-lose business venture. Consider Air Jordans—our kids want them, need them; well, that's another issue. Third-world people make them, but they are sold here. The "global economy" is based on a belief that all people are on a level playing field, which we can go wherever and be treated as we are at home. Folks, *Fantasy Island* was a television show. In reality, we have rich and poor, oppressed and oppressors, good and bad; equality is a concept of where you are in the present, with no carry over. For that reasoning, I have seen relatively few American company open and sell their products there, only rape the foreign land and people for capitalistic gains. You got to love American ingenuity.

This is the second part of the model: we the people. Yep, all of us. Now that you have been displaced by your foreign counterpart—a theoretically better worker, a smarter worker, or whatever bullshit title that corporate management puts on this—the bottom line is that you have no employment. Along with this situation, and not really grasped or cared about by greedy corporate executives, is one significant issue. You're out of work, which means you are receiving no paycheck, which means you are not purchasing goods. Let me expound on the "not purchasing" of goods. Yes, the daily necessities of food and shelter will be dealt with, though probably cut back. However, that new big-screen television, is on the back burner. No spending equals a major hole in the economic situation.

American spending and consumption have two sides, and they are similar and unique all at once. We as Americans are creatures of wants and needs. They are not the same thing but do follow the same path.

Needs are the things, such as food and shelter, we require in order to survive and we need money to buy those items. When economic climate change or degradation is a concern, the effects on needs is not so critical. Instead of steak, you may eat chicken, but, regardless, you will still eat.

Wants, on the other hand, are not required and therefore are more devastatingly affected in times of economic crisis. No paycheck equates to crisis, and the corporate sector really does not care about your personal financial Armageddon. Corporate America still wants you to spend even though you can't pay for it. To some degree, business is winning this battle. A prudent person with no viable source of income should put these unruly wants or passions on the back burner. Yeah, just like we all should watch our food intake and obey all the posted signs on our roads. Not going to happen religiously. So we charge and charge some more, play with our meager resources as we play with our new cell phones or wide screens. Eventually our wants create another issue, a bigger issue: debt. Yes, a debt that looks and probably is insurmountable to many. What is going to happen next? All signs point to something not good for the consumer and for business. Suicide and bankruptcy are not pretty actions. Yes, this dramatic; however, those actions were prevalent in the Crash of 1929, and it can happen again. The rise and fall of the American lifestyle is upon us. So where is the outsourcing going? It's as I said a pseudo-economy, a false reading of the market. Folks, we have the sub-prime mortgage fiasco all over again, but with far worst consequences.

Now back to the solutions and tactics to regain our employment and put our country back on the right track. All of us, most of us, or some of us feel that sitting on our collective asses and doing nothing is the correct choice. We feel that the problem is just too big, so why do anything? Hey, it's your life, your kid's life, the lives of your friends and family; it is all of us. Remember this: the definition of a good politician, his legacy; is one who keeps his constituents employed. In simpler terms, the economy is the lifeline of our government. With this objective met, the elected can do whatever he or she wants to whomever he or she wants. Let us begin.

Okay, I have a number of tactics, initiatives, procedures, or just things that, if done, hopefully in mass, can turn the tide. Behavior modification, a controversial term of my college years, can be applied to the business of outsourcing. I do not know why nor do I agree that the process of behavior modification is so controversial. We all use it. We all get the results from it. The process is totally holistic. No electrodes or drugs are needed, only positive and negative reinforcements toward a behavior. Business behavior can be modified with these techniques.

These are general guidelines that I can attest to. Yes, they do work. I have used them on smaller issues with very, very good results.

1. Use the power of the press. Yes, the word is most definitely mightier than the sword. Words are your weapon and the readership your army. Press, especially bad press within the corporate world, translates into less and less money, based on decreasing product sales. Do not forget the cardinal rule: it's always about money. Yes, money can buy happiness, especially when it comes to corporate management. It is a known fact that well-established products cannot rest on the past. The power of the press, together with the use of advertising, reminds us that the product still exists and

that the consumer must buy it. The positive press has an evil twin: negative press. For celebrities, the impact of the press is an absolute value: both positive and negative press is good, and only no press is bad. So be a bad girl, a party girl, a Lindsey Lohan, if you wish; yes, a train wreck is apparent, but her name is in all the media, people are talking, opinions are made, and she is not forgotten. Business, on the other hand, does not have such a vision of the press. Negative press, true or not, is the kiss of death. And that equates to less dollars, and we all know what the church of business pays homage to.

2. Go hunting, bird hunting to be more precise. I am not advocating taking your AK-47 out and killing all the CEOs and their counterparts. This would be effective, but oh so … You fill in the adjective. I am talking about the concept of bird hunting, the principles behind it. When hunting birds with a weapon that uses gunpowder, a single bullet is a waste of time. The bird is small, erratic in his flight pattern, and would be, if hit by this metal projectile, to use a morbid term, "nuked". Your catch would be nothing but feathers if any. That is why a shotgun is used. Small projectiles are launched, covering a significantly bigger area. The words that are written should be made available to all eyes. Do not use the lame words of our military to sell an impending war action with "surgical" bombs. You want everybody and anybody to read your words. These eyes have the potential to make your target very uncomfortable, and that is what you want.

3. When you make some sort of communication, written or verbal, refrain from personally abusive language. Keep it short, simple, and to the point. Calling the party you're dealing with a "fucking asshole", while it might be and usually is true, totally lessens your credibility and gives the benefit of doubt to your opponent.

4. State facts. Do not get on a soapbox and preach. Go back to the days of the dreaded "blue book" in college. Yep, the single question with multiple sub questions that had to be answered. The golden rule on all these questions is to support your answer; explain why you said what you said. A simple yes or no just doesn't cut it; you must have reasons why you went that way.

5. Remember the power of numbers. I am not going into some mathematical model, just plain and simple numbers. Yes, there is a mega-truth in the powers of numbers. Look at a pyramid scheme; yes, this has a negative connotations, but it shows that the masses make the top very wealthy. Another fine example is the Catholic religion. Now I know those of you that are wrapped up in this will despise me. Too bad—open your eyes and smell the coffee. When Catholics marry, he and she are brainwashed to produce more and more kids and to believe that any type of birth control or abortion is wrong. Why is this? Let's not go down the path of when life begins; this is not my focus. The law of numbers is. With more Catholics, there is more power, and there is more money; it's that simple. When making some sort of written communication, this is my hard and fast rule: with either letters or email, CC others. As I previously stated in concept number 2, use the "shotgun effect". The CC list can and should contain a multitude of others like agencies, newspaper, media, and other organizations—basically any and all. If you feel that they might benefit your cause, include them. What I have found is that doing this will achieve major objectives in your cause:

   - Sending a single letter to a party is an effort in futility: nothing gets done. Usually your communiqué gets put into the "circular file".

   - Including multiple CC recipients put multiple eyes on the problem. Multiple eyes mean multiple questions from people with more power than you.

Embarrassing questions are raised, and usually a positive solution to your issue will be attained. This does work; I know from personal issues I have had with businesses.

- Do not be quick to discount or eliminate names. If you have the slightest feeling that the addressee will be an asset to your cause, include them. The more the merrier.

6. Utilize organizations. This is an extension of the power of numbers. Look at AARP, an organization of people over fifty. This group of people doesn't fit into the demographics for television shows, but it works for AARP. I have had many assignments at The Hartford as an IT resource in personal lines, primarily auto insurance. AARP promotes The Hartford to its members, and well it should. The rates to AARP members are lower, which means a smaller premium for the policyholder. Further, a policyholder with the AARP version cannot be denied or lose coverage. Even if you are a terror on wheels with multiple points against your license, your policy cannot be cancelled. There are only two ways you can lose coverage: first, if you do not pay your premiums; second, if your doctor provides a statement that you are unfit to operate a motor vehicle. AARP negotiated these benefits, and The Hartford agreed. The Hartford is a major player in the auto insurance market. Of their total book of auto insurance business, AARP represents more than 70 percent of it. This is a significant piece of business that the Hartford cannot afford to lose; in other terms, it's one hell of a bargaining chip that AARP has. Another well-known company, Amazon, wants to expand their facilities into the northeast. A local town gave them tax abatements, but Amazon wants more. They will probably get it; Amazon, by its size and reputation, will work for them. Another example of numbers is Wal-Mart. I am not a big fan, but I will give credit when deserved. Wal-Mart, a large retail

conglomerate, deals with many manufacturers who want to be in their stores. Manufacturers make goods and sell goods. Selling goods at a store means that the store wants a piece of the action. The manufacturer sells the products at a wholesale cost. It is less than retail, so all parties get a piece of the pie. Wal-Mart, being so big, negotiates for lower wholesale prices and usually gets it. Why? Simple: the law of numbers.

7. Remember our elected officials. They sometimes forget—actually always forget—that we, the electorate, are their bosses. We, the lowly populace, have the power to elect or not to elect these jokers. As a side note, I wish we had a national recall option as they have in California, but we don't. This would definitely put more fear into Washington. But the power of the press and written word gets the media and pundits talking and asking the embarrassing questions. This works.

8. Never forget that it is always about the money. This is probably the strongest ally we have. Businesses hate the word boycott. This equates to decreased sales, which mean a smaller bottom line. Execs hate this. Remember several years back, a famous radio personality on WNBC and WFAN, Imus in the Morning, was booted off the New York station for comments he made about Rutgers's women's basketball team. The driving force of his expulsion was the radio sponsors pulling their ads, which meant the radio station was losing revenue. As I said, it's always about the money.

9. Consider the union. Yes, unions have a lousy history, and yes, some of their demands tend to be on the absurd side; however, using the power of numbers to fight for a single goal will get the job done.

24: Cabaret

Ah yes, a fantastic Broadway show, performed by many. I saw it on Broadway with Alan Cummings in the lead. It is a light-hearted musical set in Germany, prior to the outbreak of WWII. The emcee, played by Mr. Cummings, sings this song with the flowing lyrics: "money makes the world go around"; the words have stood the test of time, and they are as pertinent now as they were then—no, not the show's creation, but the beginning of all time. Money, in all its forms—precious metals, dollars, pounds, yen, whatever—is the common denominator.

Work is compensated by dead presidents; sports contracts are always revolving about compensation, which means money; and even contract or crime retribution comes down to dollars. Lawyers really do not care about justice, who is right or wrong. No, they care about their client. Their client paid the attorney to get him, the client, out of a position he is in. There is never an admission of guilt, nor is that ever included in the equation of justice on the pending litigation. As with most situations the "what about me?" factor is the only "justice" in the land. An auto accident occurs; the judgment is always about dollars to make it right. I can see payment for physical damages and health issues; however, punitive damages are a bonus that goes beyond making it right. A wrongful death suit is a very confusing piece of legalese. Nothing can be done to bring a dead person back to the living, so tons money will make it right. Sorry, Billy Shakespeare, the *Merchant of Venice* just doesn't cut it here. This gives credence to the idea that you are worth more dead than alive.

So the solution to this epidemic of outsourcing is the same thing that businesses covets: money. *Money* is the double-edged sword; which side will we fall on? Outsourcing will stop when the source of this cheap, bullshit line of the so-called global economy is made too costly for businesses either from lost business or when the tax man cometh to collect his pound of flesh—I mean tons of flesh. Unfortunately, this does take time. However, my basis for everything in life is that what goes around comes around. It is our task to force the issue, make that merry-go-round rotate at warp speed, by all and any means.

25: Sell Your Soul to the Devil

Got your attention. Well, back to reality, I am not a religious person, so the concept is mysterious to say the least.

Now I have bitched, with evidence and provocation, that our elected court jesters are sleeping with the enemy. So be it. However, stranger things have happened, and I like to play the lottery.

Outsourcing is here, and most likely it will stay. This does sound counterproductive to what I have said, but ground zero must be reached before we can reverse this tsunami. Packing up the garbage and shipping it back to where it came from, though very appealing, is not going to happen soon. So let's go back to the root of the problem: money. Yes, the universal cause and effect quotient, the common denominator. Money is the god of business, penicillin, and heroin, all in a neatly tied Christmas package.

Here is an additional fact that should be acknowledged by our elected: everything is done for, by, to, and with money. And this is abundantly true for our elected leaders. Our country is in a financial perfect storm, to say the least, a storm that affects and is affected by the deficit, Social Security, and the national debt. My proposal, well some would be happy and conversely, some will more than hate.

All right, I concede; this battle is too epic, too one-sided. Let corporations have all the "golden children of IT", as many as they want. The more the merrier. Now, that seems to be an abrupt change of course from what I have been saying. What a kick in the ass. Yes, wee one, this appears to be contrary to my writings; however, as Paul Harvey always said, "Now here is the rest of the story". Do not think people are so righteous and honorable; for the right money, anyone would sell his or her soul to the devil. Everything, every person, anything has a monetary price tag on it. Everybody has a price for himself or herself as a product or service. The only variable is how much. It's an interesting analogy, selling your soul to the devil; think about it. Slaves were bought and sold as commodities back in the 1800s, and business in my opinion resurrected it in the 2000s. So here's how my proposed solution to this outsourcing crisis would play out for us, the populace, using the realm of IT as a model; other areas could use it as well.

- For every non-American technical resource imported and used at our businesses, those businesses will be taxed by our government. This is in additional tax to what they are paying now. I propose $250K/resource/year ad infinitum as long as he is serving his master, I mean at the corporation. Let me show the big picture. The corporate tax addition for one hundred outsourced positions would be $250 million per year on top of existing corporate taxes.

- No grandfathering, no exemptions, no deals, nothing.

- This proposal can be done at the federal level or at the state level.

- The tax on the corporation will be reduced only when an American assumes the position.

- The benefits of this proposal:

  1. Ability to build and sustain a technological army of sorts

  2. Economic growth

  3. Education growth

4. Technology giant

5. Decrease in deficient and debts to foreign adversaries

Now, we all know how business feels about taxes. Also, we know that all are expendable when it comes to the business. On another note, if these foreign resources are that "fantastic" as advertised, this tax is a mere blip on the radar. I think not.

Yes, others countries will retaliate when their cash cow stops producing money. But we are a superpower, I have been told, and therefore not subservient to anyone. Let them eat cake, as Marie said in France.

26: Get a Bigger Hammer

For any job that is performed at work or play, there is a proper tool for the task. This simple rule has been broken oh so many times with the cry, "just get a bigger hammer!" It is true in the corporate world as well. There is a power shift in corporations from qualified IT management to incompetent business management posing as IT management. This behavior demonstrates the Peter Principle so eloquently. This concept is: *in a hierarchically structured administration, people tend to be promoted up to their "level of incompetence"*. Current business has exemplified this to the nth degree. There are many current project managers, project leaders, and directors that can barely turn their desktops on, let alone manage technical resources or understand the basics. These are but a few of the flunkies that I have met and have dealt with. The names have been omitted only out of fear of reprisal and assault.

There is, in my humble opinion, a quick but misguided class in project management that is marketed and used at our companies. I have had the experience of working under PM—project managers—who I thought were not ready to be prime time players. Non-PMs took classes in project management that gave levels like Black Belt, Green Belt, and so forth to the participants who progressed further and further in the curriculum. No, this was not a martial arts class but a pseudo-project management class. Conversations with the participants or graduates of these classes often revealed that they neither wanted nor understood these classes. These sentiments were expressed to me by them. However, toeing the company line, they were instructed to partake, and so they did. They were business folks, not technical in even the most minimal way; however, working with technical staffs, senior management deemed this educational task to be sufficient. For example, the current "fast-track" IT managers do not know the differences between online and batch systems; the bottom line is they are functionally technical illiterates. Mind you, they often have both types of systems under their departments. Go back to Finger Painting 101, please.

Current IT management cannot see the forest beyond the trees. The conversion and migration of systems is common in business and is monetarily very costly. I was at a major insurance firm working on one of these migration projects, which can really bore down to the core of this issue. To the non IT person, data looks like numbers and letters, and you would be right. However, to the IT professional, data is a very dynamic and vibrant subject, not just letters and numbers; it can tell and do a myriad of things in systems—a storyteller of sorts, like the folk singers of old. I noticed that a key data element, which was on the old system, was garbage. This data was being migrated, moved to a newer system "as is". Yes, it was the "garbage in, garbage out" phenomenon. I knew the new system was using this element as a key and that it would be vital for it to be correct. I knew the fix would be costly, but I would be derelict in my position if I did not expose the pending issue. This additional cost would be negligible compared to the cost of fixing it later. I described this issue to my incompetent leaders; I also stated that this would be an ideal time to fix this issue and provided a game plan on performing this task. I was told no way. So, as a good vendor, I shut my mouth and did what I was told. As a vendor, I am a hired gun and do what the client wants; after all, they are paying me. However, my concerns would bite him on the ass—it was just a matter of time—and it did. Following this migration project, I supported the new system and did many independent and monetarily costly marketing initiatives. Anybody who has done mass mailings, the slow mail type, knows that printing and postal costs are, shall we say, major. This same manager that

I had previously, noticed on a report that duplicate mailings with the same information were going to the same address. He posed that concern to me. I said yes, I know. The next issue he voiced was déjà vu: could we fix this issue to bring the costs down? I said yes, but it was going to be costly, very costly. I referred him back to our previous conversation about the garbage element that he did not want fixed; I said that was the issue. We did not fix the problem; it was deemed too costly.

The software sales force corresponds to used car salesmen or lawyers: they all use some truth wrapped around with tons of bullshit. Software guys throw a lot of buzzwords out, and I will not say lie but misconstrue the facts. A businessperson can hear their pitch, and it all sounds great; however, we all know if it sounds too good to be true then probably it's not. I saw this at two places. The first company brought in systems personnel to listen to the sales pitch, ask the correct questions, and challenge the sales team, and they had a significant impact on the decision to purchase the product. This went well.

Conversely, the second company had disastrous results. This second company was a defense contractor who also worked with the commercial world. A standard practice at a company who works with the military is to have some in roads into that world; they hire high-ranking retired military for that. They are handed a cushy position, thought to be not too dangerous to the business, and left to exist. Well, this token general made some IT decisions without system's help, and the IT area, once a well-oiled operation, is in the junk heap. This director made a decision, in my opinion, setting the IT operations way back. He outsourced the IT department to an IT vendor—a devastating business move. Originally the IT staff were actually tied to a business unit, work ran smoothly, business and IT management worked cohesively, and things got done. Now the consulting company, who had assumed control over IT operations, had experience and emphasis on taking over IT departments at several other major companies. One major factor of all consulting companies is billing. Yep, every person working on the consulting payroll is responsible for accounting, or rather billing, for hours on-site. Once a well-oiled operation, is now a billable nightmare.

Consider Obamacare, or the Affordable Care Act—not the bill but the web site. This is a prime example of incompetent business/IT management running a multi-hundred million dollar IT project. I do not have a crystal ball or any direct inside information on this blunder. However, I have seen the scenario play out before, and the results are always the same.

The tide of inept IT management must be replaced with IT resources: local, American, qualified resources with local IT talent. The fall is imminent, and look for major companies go on the stock market in a fire sale.

27: The Proof Is in the Pudding

My thirty-something years in IT plus the additions of my esteemed colleagues and peers have allowed me to list some examples of IT problems that do exist today or will hit in the future.

Obamacare: the website joke. I do not care what your position is on the Affordable Care Act; my focus is on the IT process, the system to enroll participants. What an expensive joke, and yes, pull your collective pants down and prepare to be "greeked", or should I pay the piper for incompetence.

Let me first state this disclaimer. Every major IT implementation that I have been a part of or have witnessed has had minor glitches; this is a "fact of IT life". However, the degree of issues that the Obamacare website release had, I have rarely seen. The following are the issues I have with this project:

Obamacare, or the Affordable Care Act

- Obama and his administration. He administered a stimulus package, and what did that do? Here we had a major IT project, and we gave the IT work to a foreign firm. Why? Nothing against the foreign firm; however, we had 8 percent unemployment. It was a no-brainer: use an American firm. And that was not the worst part: this foreign vendor had a major contingent of third-world flunkies. Yes, the incompetent offshore resources that I scream about.

- This project was an ideal picture of non-IT management running an IT project. It was stated in the media more times than I care to admit that there was not enough testing.

- I expounded on the fact previously that "your next IT boss will not have IT"; this was played out in living color. The American leading this major project had no IT expertise. As I said, open your eyes and ears—it is all there. And it is not a pretty picture.

- Specs, the ongoing argument in perpetuity. Now I have not seen or read any documentation; however, the postmortem plays out the same. Again this issue reared its ugly head.

- The press has shown a war of words and finger pointing of who is the blame. Trust me, there is enough blame to go around. Quit trying to save your own collective asses.

28: Just Because You Can

We all can go to San Francisco, proceed to the iconic Golden Gate Bridge, and jump into the water. Yes, jumping off the bridge is illegal. Suicide or attempting suicide is illegal, and, really, the victim and perpetrator are one and the same. Do you think the jumper really cares about legalities? Well, the laws say it so. However, a more poignant issue is that the distance from the bridge to the waters is high, the waters below are relatively cold, and therefore the probability of killing yourself is, shall we say, a "sure thing" as far as that goes. A prudent or mentally stable person would have other thoughts on this. I can assume that this individual falls into one of two categories. One he is mentally unstable. Or two, he is a thrill seeking junkie, who thinks he has all the pertinent facts about this death defining jump.

Just because you can do something does not mean you have carte blanche to do it. Be it law, moral, religious, or anything should prevent all things being done all the time. There is no universal law; it's case by case. I took an ethics class when I was in college many years ago. The professor posed an interesting question that prompted no less an interesting and heated discussion. The question was, is it always bad to lie? The answer had to be an unqualified yes or no, not maybe. This was a simple question with no corporate law or religious overtones for the Catholic audience, but it required a simple answer: yes or no. A lively discussion and no resolutions to the question were attained.

Another example of absolute power involves the operating of a boat. As with an auto, there are hard and fast rules, so is true in boating. However, in boating, if a situation occurs where breaking a rule is needed for your own safety, then break the rule. As you can see, the words of always and never are not cast in granite.

Now then, I have a car that has a speedometer stating that this vehicle can attain speeds of 160 mph. Impressive, an objective view of what my car theoretically can attain in terms of speed. Now, I do not know if my vehicle can actually attain the speeds on the gauge; however, I do know that it can and has broken the triple-digit barrier. How do I know this? Simple: I did it. Not a wise choice on many levels, but the knowledge that this car has the ability to attain high speeds in a relatively short time is impressive. I guess it is a macho kind of thing.

There are many people of the driving public who drive under the influence of alcohol, drugs, or both. Now, I am not in law enforcement, I am a liberal and at the same time a conservative. I do not care if individuals impaired by their vices of choice kill themselves while driving. Hey, according to my Catholic upbringing, we all have free will, so taking their life, as tragic as it is, is their choice. This is my liberal view. Conversely, if the same individuals under the same impairments are on the road with me, my friends, or family, then I want the full power of our laws to keep us out of harm's ways by any and all means.

For the most part, we all bitch and moan about tax season and the task of filling out the Form 1040 whatever suffix and attaching, if warranted, a payment check. Some individuals take this to the extreme and not even do the process—a very, very bold if stupid approach. The IRS code (IRC 61) wants us to pay our taxes on our income, no matter if we attained it by working a job or selling drugs on our local street corner; the IRS wants their fair share. As long as you do that, they, the IRS, are happy as pigs in shit. There is a larger sample of those who avoid the taxman by absence; it is the creative accounting principal. How aggressive one is on recording those figures on those many lines, well, there is no one looking over your shoulder as you fill your tax papers out. Take your chances on getting caught or being subjected to the famous audit. The IRS has its own code of justice; when you are caught, you are guilty and you must prove your innocence, as opposed to the other side where you are innocent until proven guilty. I recall an incident many years ago where I was a participant that required me to fill out some very intense financial papers. At that time, my attorney said to me that I could put anything I wanted down those papers, but if asked—and they would—then I would have to supply proof of my figures.

Just because you can doesn't make it the right choice. As I have said, I am a capitalist and a proponent of business; however, the choice of businesses today with regards to IT and the outsourcing of the associated services are bad on so many levels. A commandment of Business 101, as previously stated, is that the business is the sole responsibility unto itself; everything else is a casualty of war. So, based on that profound statement, they (being corporate management) are religiously upholding the commandment. Business is permanently and stoically in the "what about me?" mode and has extreme tunnel vision and no foresight. Business works on the here and now, though they plan for the future. Here is why this practice, behavior, or immediate corporate greed should be reversed:

- The obvious, the here and now, the no-brainer, is that Americans should have these positions that have been given to our lesser counterparts. The economic benefits are way too numerous to expound on.

- We are becoming a nation of illiterate couch potatoes. We have over-developed wrists and hands to play those video games, but what about the technology to develop them? Why spend thousands of dollars on a meaningful degree and then be turned away from the corporate sector because they are not the right race?

- Charity begins at home. So true, but I am not calling for a national welfare system but to develop and use our people. People, our people, are a national resource that should be used and developed.

- We're number one. Yes, that chant resounds at all kinds of athletic events, and it also applies at the corporate level. We did, at one time, lead the world with technology and employment; we were the envy of the entire world. That is diminishing; we are a country of users or abusers and not leaders.

- An old statement about business, "to make money you have to spend money", is a fact and rule of business that is old as dirt and as current as newest iPhone. Corporate mores that focus only on the here and now must be changed. Yes, greed is good; however, not when it is reflected on oneself instead of outside interests.

- In education, theory is good; however, the practical must also be there. Solid techies need to be well rounded in all aspects of the world.

- Do we need that nasty thing called government intervention? My view is that our elected can't get a wet dream right. However, big business has shown stupidity and greed, so maybe two wrongs do make a right. Private enterprise with respect to business practices and the stock market needs to be tempered with legislation for two reasons. First, people in general are stupid, they hear what they want, they are followers, and they go with a knee-jerk response always; they need protection from the corporate sharks. And second, we need protection from the business's insatiable and, unadulterated greed. This greed open up our economic world and turns it into the Wild Wild West.

- Technology is a brave new world. Technology is the wave of the future. Computers will be responsible for more than insurance companies and managing policies. Farming, fishing, medicine, and trucking to name a few will be enthralled with technology. We must be in the forefront.

29: Memories

The choir is singing "life is unfair". Anguish by the oldies—I give it a score of seven, Dick; it has a good beat. These profound lyrics are so very true. Probably you have heard these words spouted by your parents, grandparents, or many of your relatives and friends, but why? Does it always have to be that way? Is this the religious bullshit of penance and sacrifice one must endure to get to heaven? Question, is there a heaven, and is the converse true, a hell? Is this the same rhetoric of the Taliban suicide terrorist, that the afterlife will give you seventy-two virgins if you murder the infidels? Nice urban myths and fodder for the writers of books and movies, but truth and verification are not factually available. IT's mainstay is logic; to get C you must go through A and then B. You got to love the computer, the "black box"—everything is black and white.

The outsourcing of American labor for the sake of profits can and should be stopped. What I have said in this writing has essentially made me a terrorist of business, a socialistic medicine man, and has killed my career and the career of my wife and kids. Yeah, I am a dumb bastard who is idealistic and will make profound statements. Yes, I do make these statements. No excuse, no denial; however, I make these statements and back them up with what I see as evidence of why I say them. Well, here is the rest of the story: my wife and I have retired from the rat race commonly known as working for the man. We are financially stable and have no rug rats, yet we see that the path our corporate idiots are on will financially destroy our great country, will lead to the rise and fall of America. A tradition of trials and tribulation in the past does not mean that this path is required in the future. Yes, technology is our new frontier; it is growing and will continue to grow, either with our support or not.

There is a glimmer of light at the end of the tunnel, be it ever so faint. Our government and military are making waves that only flags made in America can be flown and only American-made uniforms can be worn by our soldiers. Do we really need to pass a law or make a statement for this? Well, it's on the table now. Also, companies are making it known that their products are being made here; maybe corporate greed is changing into nationalism.

I believe that charity begins at home. That is not to say the hell with everybody else. However, we must take care of number one first, and that is us. It's too bad these third-world nations have a mega-population issue; apparently neither keeping it in their pants nor birth control is in their behavior repertoire. Not my or your problem. I refuse to go along with "it takes a village"—you made it, you take care of it.

As I have said, this behavior by our business management must be stopped. If not, yes, the businesses will look great in the short run, but the prize will be but a mirage, as it will devour corporations in the future. Greed begets greed, and that will collapse us. The rise and fall of America, and I pledge allegiance to the flag of the (fill in the blank) will be the anthem of us if we do nothing.

30: Monday-Morning Quarterback

The day after Sunday, at work or school or wherever, we all talk about "the game". No special game, but an intense critiquing on what transpired on Sunday, especially if our team lost. This happens in person, on sports talk radio, and on all types of media. It always includes analysis of how you could have handled the situation—definitely better than the current powers that be.

Well, the game is still going. The "fat lady" has not sung her swan song. And as Yogi Berra once said, the game isn't over till it's over. There is sufficient evidence that the present management philosophy must be changed. By continuing down this path of self-destruction, this is what I see:

- Why go to an institution of higher education? The answer is simple: the "college life". But that is not a thing you want on your resume. Majoring in "beer pong" or bikiniology at spring break or racking up frequent flyers mileage going to all those games? Yep, these things will help you progress in life.

- Master the couch potato. Watching the finer aspects of *Jerry Springer* or *Jersey Shores* is so enlightening in today's world.

- Increasing your anonymity quotient. Yep, hide behind a computer, smart phone, or tablet and bully.

- Complain, complain, and complain. But to whom? We will all be in the same boat.

- "I pledge allegiance to the flag of the United States of America, and to the republic for which it stands ..." Well, the country roulette wheel is turning; where it stops nobody knows.

- Regress to becoming a third, fourth, or lesser world nation

- Become a nation, worse than we are now, of ultra-consumers and not producers.

- Lose our number-one status in technology. Basketball and baseball will survive. I guess hocking hot dogs and beer is our career path.

This is a bleak prognosis and will most certainly become reality under this "tag sale" mentality of corporate management. I heard a financial person on the television talking about entitlements. Not the entitlements our village idiots talk about in Washington but our educated souls. His take was that just because you go to college, you should not assume that you will get a job. I am going to take this on with an answer I sometimes give my wife: yes, no, maybe. Talk about noncommittal. Okay, you spend four years or so at an institution of higher learning, get a degree in finger painting. Artistically you have the finer points of this "endeavor", but really is it meaningful, needed, and if so of what value? However, a stellar degree in computer science should be molded, nurtured, and propagated into today's business climate. Yes, HAL is here to stay, to stay in earnest.

31: They Come to Take Me Away, Ha

Many people think I am looney tunes. Nothing new here. I have said and done things that may have been against public opinion or at least the pinstripes among us, only to have it be revealed later as the truth. I make no apologies and own up to what I have said. I am not a politician.

History, as I have stated countless times, yep, that bastion of documenting all events, has recorded many instances. Some of these instances that were suppressed, should have gone, as stated, on a different tack. Let us take General Douglas MacArthur. At the end of WWII, he wanted to attack North Korea and China. Yes, a major undertaking, but look at where we are today with both radical nations. MacArthur was proactive, was spot on, and held views totally opposite to Truman. He was at odds with President Truman, and although he was right, he was removed from his military position. Oh well, Harry. Give 'em hell, as you would say.

This is not my first rodeo on publicly bucking the so-called experts. I was at Aetna—you know, the people you are glad to meet. At the end of my tenure, the upper management had kind of a fire sale, selling off the property and casualty, life insurance, annuity, pensions, and real-estate lines of business. This left them with health insurance as their only line of business. I said this was crazy. Why? A common and proven business doctrine is to diversify, spread risk; this is a good and proven philosophy. Putting all your eggs in one basket gives you no safety net. I am not a person who has a Harvard MBA in his back pocket, so I was ignored as a radical. Fine; I am thick-skinned, so I just did my systems work. However, I did get vindicated several months after my radicalism. On a business talk show—you know, the ones where the educated talking heads speak about politics, business, foreign affairs, and government—a fair number if not all agreed with me. Aetna, they said, should not have sold off these lines of business. Oh well, privately I was laughing and patting myself on the back.

Now to present times. Yes, I am vehemently against outsourcing! Not just for the obvious, but for many other stated reasons. We are a nation that is having a fire sale on employment. Why? "Take care of number one" and "charity begins at home" are my mottos. There are no positive gains from this action. I totally refute our elected with their supposedly sound economic policies on why outsourcing is good. Why? That is simple: they are all habitual liars looking out for their own agenda. No, I am not advocating the isolationism that was rampant in the post-WWI years. However, I am not in favor of sustaining and building foreign economies. This is so non-Christian. Yes, it is not fair. It is cruel to ignore our fellow man. However, and this is a big *however*, business is warfare! And war does have casualties! Make those casualties anybody but us.

Several years ago I was part of a volatile conversation about socially conscious investing. Their view was very sympathetic to countries, peoples, or economies that were exploited. Honorable, but not capitalistic. My take on this was it was legal, it was making me economically better off, and the professionals were saying we should make these companies part of our portfolio. So I did. This tactic relates to spending thousands on education and not recouping your investment—the ROI factor as it applies to individuals. It is very honorable and philanthropic to learn a therapeutic trade like finger painting for the handicapped. Yes, it's good for soul and mind. However, you cannot sustain yourself economically with this. The ROI factor has not been satisfied. If you do this, fine, but don't cry for me, Argentina, when you can't pay the rent.

Writing and re-reading my last several statements makes me think that outsourcing is good. Hey, I am a capitalist. Yes, I am a capitalist, but I am also a realist. My analytical experience and exposure trained me to ask questions, look at all the possible scenarios, evaluate the positive and negatives results of an action, and determine a path that is correct for my task at hand. So while outsourcing offers good short-term gains, long-term they are abysmal. I will forego the short-term euphoria for the bigger piece of the pie.

As my parting words, we are doing more harm to our nation than we are doing economically well with the false philosophy of outsourcing employment under the auspices of a global economy. Bottom line: *it's always about the money*, nothing more or less. This is my mantra, the means do not justify the end!